REVIEWS

"The biggest challenge we all face is figuring out what matters, and what doesn't -- really fast. Baha and Margaret Habashy have built the ultimate Anti-Overload tool! Use it, enjoy it, learn from it, and relax...They've got the cure you're seeking."

Bill Jensen, Author,
Simplicity Survival Handbook, What Is Your Life's Work?

"From Overload to Balanced Living" is a practical and powerful polemic confronting the problem of imbalance in one's life. Rather than offering pat solutions, Baha and Margaret Habashy guide the reader into a different way of thinking about one's relationship to the urgent or the important and the freedom acquired by recognizing and choosing the latter."

Dr. R. Bruce Bickel, President,
Transformational Leadership Group

"This is a wonderfully uplifting and practical book to help people in any work environment today. I enjoyed reading about the experiences of people just like me and others I work with, find success in using these tools. The book is also filled with great exercises to help the reader implement the suggested tools for success. I highly recommend it to anyone feeling the pressure of life today."

Patricia J. Hutchings, Author, Managing Chaos

"When I was asked to read "Overloaded", I said "Oh no, another self help book...I'm way too busy for that." I am very glad I read it. It helped me remember what my priorities are and should be. I especially liked the chapter that helps you handle the email and voice mail traps we fall into. That alone can save me an hour a day. Thanks Baha and Margaret!"

Orgad Gratch, CEO, TGO Consulting Inc.

"Baha and Margaret Habashy have a passion for helping people become less overloaded. They collected essential wisdom on the subject from a wide variety of sources and added their own unique perspective. This book is packed with excellent advice. Anyone who puts just a few of the ideas into practice will benefit greatly. Read it, take action, and experience the difference!"

Mark Ellwood, Author, Cut the Glut of E-Mail

"Knowledge workers, managers and leaders today are faced with unprecedented challenges in maintaining life-work balance. 24-7 accessibility, information overload, and corporate demands have turned the career marathon into a forty year sprint. This book uniquely offers strategies and practical solutions to all three of these challenges. I highly recommend it."

Bruce D McAlpine, President, Fulcrum Search Science Inc.

"This book has great value to those who are experiencing the "Baptism of Fire" in our high-stress world. It provides support to those who believe that a "good life" embraces "good work ethic" and the satisfaction of achieving in the work environment while enabling us to get the comfort of being a caring person in one's personal life as well."

Steven A. Huesing, Editor and Publisher,
Healthcare Information Management and Communication

"We are at the confluence of a river of new business technologies that straddles us with work wherever we go, and a sea of endless information. Staying afloat requires discipline and pragmatic rules. Success requires that we are able to discern wheat from chaff. "Overloaded?"-will help you chart your course through these challenging times."

Randolph Kahn, ESQ, Author-- Information Nation-
Seven Keys to Information Management Compliance

"Information overload impacts us all. Many of us do not realize the extent to which our health, family, job and relationships are under attack. In this book, Baha & Margaret Habashy not only give us a wake-up call, but suggest ways of controlling the information flow by controlling the routes it travels. A must read for those who want to regain control of their lives."

Harold Taylor, Author of Making Time Work For You

"As a productivity consultant and professional speaker, I have extensively studied the negative impact of information overload on personal productivity. This practical book presents a unique approach to help employees control overload by filtering and managing the sources of information overload. Read it, apply it and tell others about it."

Laura Stack, Author, Leave the Office Earlier

"Prior to reading this book, when someone would ask me, how do you spend your free time, I always replied: I do not have any free time...Overloaded? offers simple solutions on how to manage your overloaded, stressful, multitasking world. Amazingly, from now on - I do have "free time" marked in my daily agenda..... which I am sure will help in making me a happier, healthier and a more relaxed person."

Dorota Liszewski, Project Manager,
Gamma-Dynacare Medical Laboratories

"The key to excellence is focus. The relentless adversary to excellence is distraction and overload is the most lethal weapon. The practical concepts and strategies crystallized in this book will equip the reader to focus and will empower each person to take control of their pursuit of excellence."

Monty Page, President, All Components Inc.

OVERLOADED?

FROM OVERLOAD
TO BALANCED LIVING

TAKING CONTROL OF WORK AND
INFORMATION OVERLOAD

BAHA HABASHY &
MARGARET HABASHY

This publication is designed to provide accurate and authoritative information in regard to the subject matter. The authors and the publisher are not engaged in rendering legal, psychological, or other professional service. If professional advice or assistance is required, the services of a competent professional person should be sought.

Published by Integrity+ Consulting, 24 Dewitt Court, Markham, Ontario, Canada L3P 3Y3

Phone: (905) 294-0380

FAX: (905) 294-7084

E-mail: info@integrity-plus.com

Please contact the publisher for volume ordering at discounted pricing and for comments or review requests

Library and Archives Canada Cataloguing in Publication

Habashy, Baha, 1942-
Overloaded? : from overload to balanced living
: taking control of work and information overload / Baha Habashy, Margaret Habashy.

Includes bibliographical references and index.
Also available in electronic format.

ISBN 0-9736493-2-1

1. Knowledge workers--Time management. 2. Information resources management. 3. Quality of work life. 4. Filing systems.
I. Habashy, Margaret, 1948- II. Integrity+ Consulting. III. Title.

HF5548.85.H32 2004a 650.1 C2004-906367-7

Authors:
Baha Habashy
Margaret Habashy

A Publication of
Integrity+ Consulting
24 Dewitt Court
Markham, Ontario
Canada, L3P 3Y3

Phone: (905) 294-0380
info@integrity-plus.com

Dedication

This book is dedicated to all those who have touched our lives making us what we are today.

TABLE OF CONTENTS

Acknowledgements

This book would not have happened if it were not for the many people whose lives have helped shape our convictions and thoughts. Some of them have given us the privilege of sharing their thoughts and experience with you. Where appropriate, you see them referenced on the following pages. Here we wish to acknowledge our appreciation for their contributions:*

- Ms. Kate Agnew, Operations Manager
- Mr. Gerry Baranecki, People Manager
- Ms. Pat Clinch, Director Organizational Development
- Ms. Grace Cunningham, Manager, Human Resources
- Ms. Marie Darling, Executive Assistant
- Ms. Margie Eastwood, Coordinator, Provincial Information Management
- Dr. Rick Fenton, Strategist, Futurist
- Ms. Shelley Fletcher, Communications Director
- Mr. Ross Graham, Manager, Corporate Taxation
- Ms. Rebecca Habashy, Software Sales Professional
- Mr. Noel Habashy, University Admissions Counselor
- Ms. Donna Johnston, People Manager
- Mr. Paul Kim, Manager, Finance
- Rev. Ernest LaFont, Pastor, Police Chaplin
- Ms. Karen MacDonald, Regional Director, Quality and Education
- Ms. Susan Malenica, Regional Director, Business Development
- Ms. Dale McErlean, Finance Manager
- Mr. John McGarry, President and Chief Executive Officer
- Ms. Nada Pavic, Business Development Manager
- Ms. Joelle Perez, Finance Projects Leading Manager
- Mr. John Ramdeen, Finance Executive, Global Services
- Ms. Andrea Seymour, VP and Chief Information Officer
- Mr. Doug Stirling, Director of Corporate Accounting
- Ms. Cathy Ward, Manager, Human Resources
- Mr. Jim Wright, Operation Executive

- For our children and family members, your compliments, though often biased, are most appreciated.
- Above all, for our God and Lord, for the simple talents you have entrusted to us, we give you all our thanks and honor.

** Contributors' comments are not a reflection of the opinions of the corporations with which they are affiliated. For this reason their corporate affiliations are not listed.*

INTRODUCTION

- Overloaded like Me?
- Do You Know a Jim, Janet, or Trudy?
- How To Use This Book

Introduction

Overloaded? *Our objective is to help you take control of your overloaded world, improve your effectiveness, and reverse the negative impact of work and information overload. While our focus is on helping leaders and knowledge workers cope with work related stresses, the principles you will find in this book can bring balance to overloaded personal lives as well.*

We have three foundational statements that form the premises on which this book was created. Our hope is that you agree with these statements as they will become cornerstones on which this book will seek to help you improve your effectiveness and help you take control of work and information overload. Here are our foundational statements:

- ✓ **First:** We believe that given proper motivation, most of us would like to contribute the highest possible value to those who are important to us and to society. This book provides you with facts that will motivate you to always seek ways to improve your value contribution to your corporation, society, and those who are important to you.
- ✓ **Second:** We believe that all of us deserve the best rewards possible for the value that we contribute. This book provides you with thoughts and tips to help you significantly improve the rewards you receive for the value you deliver.
- ✓ **Third:** We believe that most leaders and knowledge workers feel overloaded and undervalued and that has to change. **This book offers you tools that can help you change, if and when you choose to change**.

Overloaded like Me?

My wife says that this cartoon is a picture of me, in a previous life. There is a great deal of truth about this. For one, I used to have a full head of hair and I have pictures to prove it!

I also used to drink 11 to 14 cups of coffee a day. This is the reason why the idea of a coffee IV seems appropriate. With my type "A" personality, I was addicted to the hurried life. Everything I did had to be done NOW, rushed, or as soon as possible.

You see, for over 25 years of my life I lived in what I would call the "hyperactive, fast moving, ever changing, totally uncertain information technology world." I worked for global giants and giants that exist no more.

By most standards I was very successful and made a great deal of money. But in August of 1999 my doctor told me that unless I changed my lifestyle and work habits he did not want to see me any more. You see, about ten years earlier, I was diagnosed with a painful condition called fibromyalgia - a chronic, transient severe pain syndrome that is highly aggravated with stress. Fibromyalgia is also associated with sleep disorder. When I went to the hospital for a sleep study the doctor found that I had less than ten minutes of restful sleep in an eight-hour study. Plus, I had an average of twenty-eight episodes of sleep apnea per hour!

So as you can see with no sleep, lots of pain and stress, I am pictured with bulging eyes and grinding teeth. You can imagine what I was like when I got home from work in the late evenings!

Yes, this is my story. To a great extent this book is a reflection of my life journey and the life journey of a faithful wife who stood by me for over thirty years. I must confess that I have not fully applied all the good advice given in this book. Yes, I am still a "work in progress". My sincere hope is that our story can save someone the risk and the painful consequences that I still carry.

Baha Habashy, Author

Before you invest your time reading this book we would like to make sure it is for you.

- Do you feel overloaded?
- Are you ready to make changes in your life priorities and habits?
- Are you concerned about someone who seems to be overloaded?

If you answered yes to any of the above questions, then this book is for you. The following chapters will give you a framework that has helped many professionals improve their effectiveness, gain higher rewards, and reverse the negative impact of work and information overload. This book will introduce you to people who share their comments with the hope that it may be of help to you. Also, you will benefit from the experience and advice of successful people living in an overloaded world without giving in to its destructive patterns.

Do You Know a Jim, Janet, or Trudy? *

It was 6:35 PM. *Jim had just walked out of a meeting with a pile of papers and a long "To Do" list. Now he knew why his boss asked him to come to this Senior Management meeting. Jim's name was not on the agenda. He always seemed to get dragged into these meetings at short notice. "It is going to be a short meeting and there's nothing to worry about," his boss had said. Jim was flattered by the many compliments showered on him during the meeting.*

He agreed that he was the best choice to get jobs done but work demands seemed to be endless. He had been working fifty to eighty hour weeks for the past two years. His boss had been asking him to take time off while at the same time piling new responsibilities on him!

** Jim, Janet, and Trudy are fictitious names and stories but exemplify situations facing many people today.*

Now he was very tired and had a splitting headache along with neck pain. His mind raced back to the events of the last few months. Business travel had taken him away from his family far more than he liked. He had promised his kids Justin, 11, Jill, 7, and Joe, 6, that he would be more consistent in attending school and sports events this year but here he was at the office thinking of the number of soccer games he had missed.

Jim felt like a sucker as he picked up the phone to call Janet, his wife. He had to tell her that he would not be home for supper. Janet was gracious in her response but the manner in which she hung up the phone spoke louder than words.

Struggling with his thoughts, Jim glanced at the flashing phone message system. As he picked up the receiver to check his voice mail, an idea came to his mind. "I know what I should do," he said to himself...

***At 6:40 PM** Disappointed by Jim's phone call, Janet collapsed on the chesterfield wondering what to make for dinner ... feeling guilty about not having a good dinner for the kids. Yet, she was utterly exhausted. Lately she felt more like a single mom. For her part, she had been very patient with Jim's work habits. While Jim was away she played both mom and dad filling in the gap. Some days she felt that this was more than she could handle...*

Driving kids to school, keeping house, and having a demanding job required eighteen working hour days. Her mother used to help a great deal until she fell down and needed hip surgery. Now she understood what it meant to be part of the sandwich generation. An overwhelming sense of responsibility for her own children and a need to offer care for her aging parents were more challenging than she had ever experienced before.

Janet knew it was late for the children's supper but she was totally unmotivated to move from the chesterfield. Then she thought, "Why don't we surprise Jim?" Just then the phone rang. She did not feel like speaking to anyone. She would rather think of something creative to do with Jim and the kids. The persistent phone ring called her to finally answer.

"Honey", the voice said. "Why don't you get the kids ready? I'll come by and we can go to the Pizza Palace for dinner and then I'll come back and finish my work."

It is about 5:45 AM*. As usual, Trudy was up early hoping to miss the traffic jam on her one-hour drive to work. Looking at herself in the mirror she wondered at the face that stared back at her. At thirty-five, the face in the mirror looked much older and less optimistic than the person Trudy wished she could see.*

Images of past years raced through her mind ... days of fun and laughter. Her friends had stopped calling. They seldom found her at home or if she was in, she was too exhausted to join them anyway. Her family understood her busyness. As a single woman she loved her niece and nephews but she had missed all their birthdays this year.

"Who are you anyway?" Trudy asked the woman in the mirror. The response from the mirror came back quickly. ***"This is Trudy Jackson, Customer Services Manager at XYZ Limited. Please leave me a message and I will call back as soon as possible."***

Trudy looked at the tired woman in the mirror and decided, "No, I have a choice. I am still in charge of my life. I will make changes."

That morning as Trudy walked into the office a senior VP, Mr. Don Matthews, met her in the hallway. "Good morning, Trudy. Do you have a minute?" he said. Leading her to his office he closed the door, looked at her firmly and said. "Trudy, I have been watching you lately and I am not very pleased with what I see. You hold a very important role in this organization and I cannot afford any risks in managing you as a vital resource." At that, Trudy began to weep. She was totally unprepared for the rebuke.

"Trudy, you are under a great deal of stress. We need you here. But we need you healthy and well. We cannot afford to have you burn out on us. You have been taking on a whole lot more lately because we have been asking you to so. We do not know how much you can handle. You are the only one who

knows your limits. Please, take care of yourself and have more balance in your life or I will have to make the changes for you."

Trudy looked at him in surprise. There was gentleness in his eyes that she had not recognized before. She believed that he cared about her and that he meant what he said. A wave of relief swept over her.

As she wiped away her tears she looked at him and said with new determination, "Well, I want to take today off. I am going to pick up my niece, go shopping and have lunch at the Children's Village."

"Good for you!" said Mr. Matthews as he shook her hand firmly and said, "Remember, I'll be watching you!"

Do You Know a Jim, Janet, or Trudy? In the workplace today there are many people like Jim, Janet, and Trudy who are overloaded. Fortunately, there is a growing number of Mr. Matthews as well. There are business leaders who genuinely care and realize that corporate future is highly dependent on the well-being of its good people. We are also glad to note that in our experience there are many who choose to search for the balanced life and have found it - many who choose to make a balanced life a priority and in the process have found a life that is more effective.

This book is for people who feel overloaded and seek to have a more meaningful and effective life. This book is about people - successful people living in an overloaded world without surrendering to its negative impulses.

While other books profile celebrities and famous people, we reference the experiences of people like you and me. People who face the same daily stresses you face. Through this book we will introduce people we have encountered as we walked and worked in a variety of endeavors. With stories, advice and opinions we would like you to meet people who have touched our lives and helped us, or people who have allowed us to touch their lives and help them through our **"Overcoming Work and Information Overload"** workshop.

While the friends we reference in this book may not consider themselves as heroes or conquerors, we consider them winners who have decided not to surrender to the destructive patterns of our overloaded world. With their permission we refer to them by name and title to help you relate to their roles and responsibilities.

Good or bad, I inherited many of my personal traits from my parents. I am a perfectionist; I got this from my mom. I am also a workaholic. This I get from my dad. I started my first career four years ago in a large, international technology corporation. I found the business world a fertile soil for my perfectionist, workaholic nature and I thrived in it. Working seventy to eighty hour weeks became a normal lifestyle for me. I admit I enjoyed the adrenalin rush provided by this fast paced project oriented world.

One day a senior executive in our corporation had a candid talk with me. He explained that I would be of greater value to the corporation and myself if I had more balance in my life. He gave me some good thoughts regarding my career and work life balance. His advice gave me courage to examine my priorities and work habits.

Recently I made a career change within the same company, for which I am very glad. Today, I am developing new skills; I am sleeping better, and I am on my way to a more balanced life.

Rebecca Habashy, Software Sales Professional

How to Use This Book

You are uniquely equipped to handle the overload problem in your own unique way. This resource book is structured so its content can be tailored to your own special needs. Use its tools with creativity to create your own solutions. Practice the tips suggested for ongoing improvement. This is a resource book. As such, it is a collection of material that you can use and modify to meet your own personal needs.

The following lists possible ways that you may use this book:

1. You can enjoy reading this book chronologically and apply its lessons as you go along.
2. Read it as an exercise book, reading one section at a time and giving yourself enough time to apply what you learn in each section before moving on to the next section.
3. Examine the table of contents and refer to a section that appeal to you and begin to learn what to do and practice what you should.
4. Skim through the pages reading the experiences and advice of successful people. As you read apply their thoughts and advice to your own life.
5. Read the practical tips and do the exercises provided in most sections and act upon them as you see best.
6. Examine the templates provided and use them as a guide or use the templates as an example and make your own templates using common office software tools.
7. Use the book as a discussion tool to coach others facing the overloaded world.

Whatever you do, make it your own. The ideas presented in this book are like a set of "Lego" blocks. Use them to develop your own model. Revisit them to enhance and reshape your model to meet your changing world. This book is designed to be a resource that you can refer to again and again. At all times remember, "The goal is progress, not perfection. So have fun."

Symbols: Here are some of the symbols that we have provided to guide you:

 this icon *or a small photograph indicates a statement or advice provided by a successful person whom we had the privilege of meeting and/or working with through our "Overcoming Work and Information Overload" workshops. Their story or comments are not the opinions of their corporations. For this reason their corporate affiliation is not listed.*

This icon Indicates an exercise that you can practice to help you develop your overload management skills. Where appropriate, a template will be referenced or provided to help you.

T This shaded capital "T" indicates a Template. Templates provide simple structures or processes to help you write your thoughts so you can **"SEE"** your thoughts, understand them clearly, and explain them to the important people around you.

Summary

✓ Most of us desire to deliver the highest value to our society and our important people. We hope this book will motivate you to do so.

✓ You deserve the best rewards possible for the value you deliver. We believe this book can help you to improve your rewards significantly.

✓ Most leaders and knowledge workers feel overloaded and undervalued. Through these pages you will learn how to change, **if you choose**.

✓ Today, many business leaders realize that corporate welfare is interrelated to the well-being of its good people.

✓ You have a choice. You can take control. We hope that this book will motivate you to make the right choice.

✓ We will give you a framework that has helped many professionals improve their effectiveness, gain higher rewards, and reverse the negative impact of work and information overload.

✓ In this book, we will introduce you to individuals who share their experiences and practical advice with the hope that it may be of help to you. These are successful people living in an overloaded world without giving in to its destructive patterns. **Yes, like them, you can do it.**

PART ONE:

STATE OF THE KNOWLEDGE WORKER

- Overloaded? Why?
  - A Cause for Work Overload
  - A Cause for Information Overload
  - How Do You Feel Today?
  - Your Overload Gauge
- What Does the Future Hold?
  - Supply and Demand for Talented Workers
  - Supply and Demand for Information
  - Improvement Indicators
  - The Personal Knowledge Management Framework

Part One – State of the Knowledge Worker

Are You a Knowledge Worker? *If you earn your primary living by processing information into knowledge and applying this knowledge to the world around you, then you are a knowledge worker. Welcome to the overloaded world!*

The industrial revolution transformed the manufacturing world and the work processes of those who earned their living making parts and products based on physical labor. The information revolution multiplied the sources of raw material available for knowledge workers without significantly changing the thinking process of those who make their living based on intelligent decision-making choices.

In this section we will examine the present state of the knowledge worker, as well as the balance of supply and demand for talent in the marketplace. Further, we will examine some of the future opportunities and challenges the knowledge worker will face.

1 – What Are the Causes and Symptoms of Overload?

What Are the Causes And Symptoms of Overload? *"Diagnose before you prescribe." Before you look for ways to reverse the negative impact of work and information overload, it is important to understand its causes. It is helpful to identify your most pressing overload symptoms.*

Did they lie to us? A few years ago, some economists and sociologists predicted that we would be working less. They told us that we would be working 3 or 4 days a week. They told us that our main problem would be to find enough leisure activities to fill our idle time. What happened to these predictions?

Today, people like you are suffering from work overload with no end in sight. In our changing environment the industrialized world has raced to a knowledge-based economy like a train out of control.

This race was fuelled by technological achievements that made it easier to create exchange and accumulate more information than we ever dreamed possible. This, in turn, has created "**information overload**" or should we call it "**work overload**"?

You and I are called "knowledge workers" because our economic value is tied to our ability to process information, make choices and take actions based on the knowledge we create as we process the information we accumulate. In so doing we are expected to share our knowledge with our information exchange partners through a varicty of media. Yes, you and I are called "knowledge workers" suffering from work and information overload.

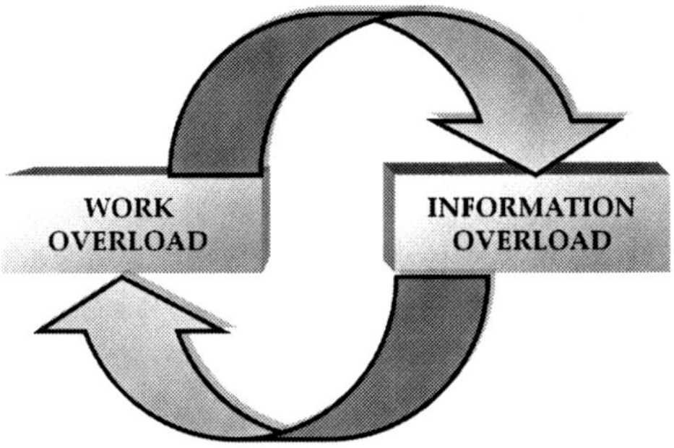

Interdependency, Work, and Information Overload

"Chicken and the Egg" Question

What comes first? Does information create work or does work create information? Does work overload create information overload or is it the other way around? The answer may vary from one person to the other. One common fact is that in our knowledge based economy, work overload and information overload are highly interlinked and interrelated. We cannot solve one problem unless we manage the other. Whether it be in our offices or at home performing simple domestic tasks, the amount of information that we have to deal with is often overwhelming.

Today we are plagued by a culture of immediacy. Technology that was supposed to help us has fueled the craving for speed and unrealistic expectations. This seems to drown our need for timely reflection.

Mr. John McGarry, President and Chief Executive Officer

Causes for Work Overload

The market place is challenging at best. Corporate leaders are driven by the need for growth. Shareholders demand it and market analysts expect it. Added to this, is the fact that corporate management has become very complex. In a diversified, global company like mine, we manage the business based on a variety of views. In matrix management we each have several masters who may have conflicting demands. All of this often creates demands that outstrip available resources. This is a key cause for overload.

Mr. Jim Wright, Operation Executive

When sociologists and economists told us that we would be working only three or four days a week and that we would have more leisure time than we could handle, they underestimated **"the law of diminishing returns"**. What is that, you say? Simply put, it means that **"the more we have, the less we are satisfied."** We want more of what we have and crave what we do not have.

To demonstrate this, consider our growing attraction for bigger and bigger homes. As we move to bigger homes, along comes the need for more and different stuff to fill these bigger homes. Yes, we are victims of our desire to keep up with the Joneses in our bigger and better neighborhood.

Or, please consider the love North Americans have had with the automobile. Instead of one family car, two cars seem to be the norm. And when our kids became teens we wanted three or four cars to meet our growing wants, not needs. We demanded more options and choices in our buying frenzy for bigger, gas guzzling automobiles. Suppliers responded to our desire for more choices. Our car dealerships became auto-malls filled with more brands, models and options than we could imagine.

Our grocery stores became supermarkets. Our markets became shopping malls and gallerias. The growing options list goes on to include everything from movies to home theatres.

Our holiday is no longer a visit to Grandma or to Aunt Betty. The options include sport camps, cruises or an all-inclusive experience in some far away resort.

Please do not misunderstand us. There is nothing wrong with this. There is nothing wrong with seeking the best lifestyle we can have, as long as we agree that the price has to be paid. Our growing demand for goods and services means we have to work more to pay for what we want. Our demand generates opportunities for others to work harder so they can pay for their own growing demand. And the song goes on and on.

Manipulative advertising and easy credit fuel our buying desires. The result is that we work harder and harder to pay more and more for what we have and what we crave. No, they did not lie to us when they told us that we would be working less. They underestimated our strong appetite for more of the "good" life. They underestimated the power of the **"law of diminishing returns"**.

Becoming a workaholic started with my childhood. As a military man, my father told us that we always had to do more than what is expected, and deliver much more than what was demanded. I grew up a doer and a caretaker.

Later, as a mother I took care of my family, as a branch manger I brought coffee and meals for my staff. This I carried into my sales career with demanding clients and ever growing sales targets. Whatever the target, I had to beat it. I had to be the best.

I knew I should change, but at my age "It's hard to teach an old dog new tricks". Concerns for my high blood pressure were easily overshadowed by customer calls and the attraction of commission checks.

One day, in a business meeting, I collapsed. When I recovered in the hospital doctors told me I had a brain aneurysm and I was lucky to be alive.

Returning from my sick leave I made significant changes and I am glad I did. I had to change. You see my doctor told me, if not careful, the next time he sees me, I could be in a casket.

By the way, while on my four month sick leave I noted something interesting; without me, the lives of those I cared for did not collapse and my business did not suffer much.

Ms. Nada Pavic, Business Development Manager

Looking strategically at the overload problem, we need to see beyond the symptoms. Here I can identify two causes. The first is my perception of the expectations of others. The second cause is the issue of personal identity and self esteem as well as how I react to the expectations placed upon me. Once we deal with these two underlying causes and take control of them the rest is symptomatic of overload, not necessarily causes.

Dr. Rick Fenton, Strategist, Futurist

We hope the above has helped you understand some of the key causes for work overload. Now let's consider some of the causes of information overload.

Causes for Information Overload

May we suggest that we have two similar health problems in our society? The first problem is the problem of overeating. Food is advertised and glamorized to us; we overeat and carry the consequences. In a similar way, we have become addicted to having too much information.

You see, our minds were created to handle information in a similar way as we handle food. We are expected to take food into our bodies in reasonable quantities. As we digest the food we turn it into energy that is used as we perform our duties and bring value to our society.

Some time ago we used to say, "Information is power". The truth is that information has no power at all. **Information** in itself has no value until it is digested through the learning process and changed into **knowledge**. Knowledge in itself has little value until it is related to the outside world in a timely and proper manner in what is called **wisdom**. Diagram 1 illustrates what we call the balanced information-processing model. **Information digested through the learning process gains its true value when it is related to the outside world in a proper and timely manner as wisdom**.

In our hurried, knowledge based world, information is thrown at us in large quantities so we do not have time to digest it properly. We tend to act in haste and wisdom falls by the wayside. This is what is called overload. Diagram 2 seeks to illustrate this reality.

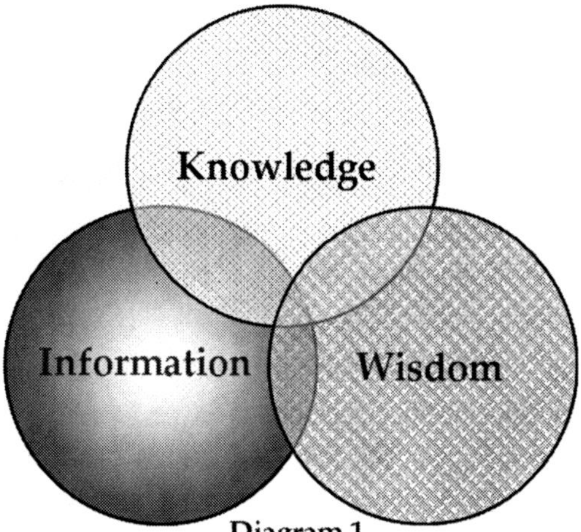

Diagram 1
Balanced Information Processing Model

In his excellent book, *The Overload Syndrome: Learning to Live within Your Limits,* Dr. Richard Swenson illustrates this overload crisis in an interesting way. We all like our doctors to be well informed and keep up with medical research. Right? Well, the author quotes Dr. Octo Barnett who writes "If the most conscientious physician were to attempt to keep up with the literature by reading two articles per day, in one year this individual would be more than eight hundred years behind."[1] The reason is that we publish almost half a million medical papers annually.[2]

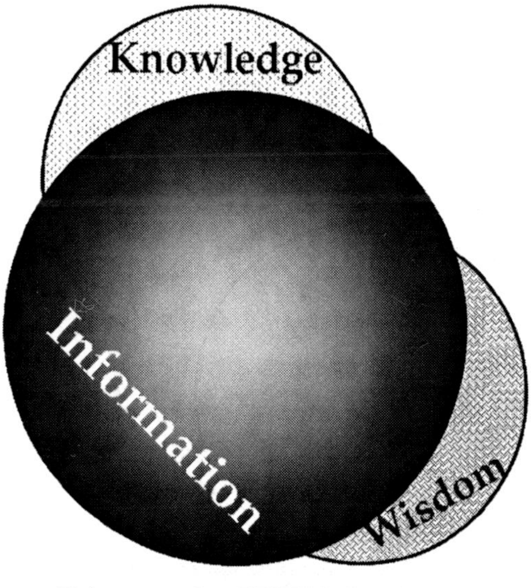

Diagram 2 - OVERLOAD

Now, wisdom suggests that doctors should spend more time with patients helping them to take control of their own care plan. Regretfully, under time pressures, it is much easier for the doctor to prescribe the latest drug based on the information he or his patient received through the TV or Internet. The result is that in North America we have the most overmedicated and drugged population in the world.

This problem of information glut or information indigestion is not limited to our physician's office. It is evident in our workplace as well as in our homes. Our minds have become the proverbial INBOX for meaningful and meaningless data. In our homes, children and adults are suffering the consequences of too much TV, video games and loud music. In the workplace, paper, e-mail, phone, and back-to-back meetings have become common causes for information indigestion.

How Do You Feel Today?

The following table will help you identify some of what are now referred to as "information anxiety symptoms." Take a moment and mark the symptoms you can relate to and how often you experience these symptoms.

Examine the items you marked as "Quite often" and mark the top two. Prioritize them as A, B based on the ones which concern you the most or give you the most stress. Later, as we discuss some solutions, thoughts, and tips try to relate them to the critical symptoms you identified.

Please note: We are not psychologists or psychiatrists and this is not a clinical diagnostic tool. If you have a feeling of anxiety that persists, you should seek appropriate professional help.

Information Anxiety Symptoms

Do you relate to these symptoms or feelings? If you do, indicate how often →→→→	Quite Often	Some times	Seldom
1. Feeling overwhelmed, flooded or claustrophobic			
2. Forgetfulness, hard to recall details			
3. Difficulty finding information, workspace totally disorganized			
4. Inability to make decisions, procrastinating far more than usual or ever before			
5. Irritability and feeling "edgy" especially with family members and those closest to me			
6. Resentment of voice mail, e-mail, and meetings, especially when the sources are friends or family members			
7. Chronically talking about not keeping up or always saying, "I am very busy."			
8. Feeling guilty over being behind			
9. Giving time and attention to low priority matters while knowing that you have more important things to do			
10. Thinking others understand all that you do not comprehend			
11. Fear of saying "No" and "I do not know."			
12. Compromised social and family life			

The Overload Gauge

In the following table we provide you with another gauge that has helped many of our workshop participants. We call it "**The Overload Gauge**". This gauge has two functions:

A. It will help you **identify and prioritize the causes** for information overload so you can focus on them as you progress in reading this book.

B. It will provide you with a yardstick to gauge your progress as you implement some of the solutions we discuss.

Please note that this gauge reflects the various parts of the solution we will discuss later. We call it the **Personal Knowledge Management Framework**. Each section of the gauge has six or seven statements.

1. Indicate to what extent you agree or disagree with each statement.
2. Add and write the score and subtotal for each segment
3. Add and write the total of all segments as your overall total.

Now you have a yardstick to guide you. Examine your gauge frequently to track your progress.

The Overload Gauge

To what extent do you agree with the following statements? (5=Totally Agree & 1=Totally Disagree)	**I TOTALLY Agree←→ Disagree**				
Filtering System					
1. I have no **control** on the amount of voice mail, e-mail, meetings, and interruptions or material I receive.	5	4	3	2	1
2. People place **urgent** demands on my life.	5	4	3	2	1
3. My roles and responsibilities cover many **subjects** and are hard to classify.	5	4	3	2	1
4. When invited to attend meetings I am not always clear on what I am expected to **be and/or do**.	5	4	3	2	1
5. I often give up my **personal life** in order to keep up with all I have to do.	5	4	3	2	1
6. I do not have clearly documented personal **goals** that relate to my personal and corporate roles.	5	4	3	2	1
7. I treat all **people** equally; it is hard for me to define who is more important.	5	4	3	2	1
Sub –Total: Filtering System Score→					

The Overload Gauge (Continued)

To what extent do you agree with the following statements? (5=Totally Agree & 1=Totally Disagree)	I TOTALLY Agree←→ Disagree				

Input System

8. By end of day, my **e-mail** in box usually has more than 10 items.	5	4	3	2	1
9. At the end of most days I have **voice mail** to which I should have responded.	5	4	3	2	1
10. I feel guilty if I have not responded to my **calls**.	5	4	3	2	1
11. On an average 70% of the time I spend in **meetings** is unproductive.	5	4	3	2	1
12. I find taking notes in **meetings** stressful.	5	4	3	2	1
13. I get too many unscheduled meetings or **interruptions** per day.	5	4	3	2	1
14. My in basket usually has **papers** that are more than 48 hours old.	5	4	3	2	1
Sub –Total: Input Systems Score→					

Filing System

15. I feel I need more **workspace.**	5	4	3	2	1
16. More than 70% of my **desk** is often covered by papers.	5	4	3	2	1
17. On an average it takes me more than one minute to find an important document in my **paper files**.	5	4	3	2	1
18. On an average it takes my boss or my associates more than three minutes to find an important document in my **filing system**.	5	4	3	2	1
19. On an average it would take me more than 30 seconds to find an item in my **electronic or e-mail files.**	5	4	3	2	1
20. I am often at least one week behind on my **reading.**	5	4	3	2	1
Sub –Total: Filing Systems Score→					
Total All Segments Score→					

As you examine your answer to the Overload Gauge, note the segment of the gauge where you rated the highest score. In response to your need this book is structured in sections similar to the three parts of the Overload Gauge. In addition, the chapters respond to the highlighted words in the above Overload Gauge statements.

Later, as you read more of the solutions provided ask yourself, "**How will this help me improve my Overload Gauge score?**" Our hope is that you will have a tool to help you prioritize the area most needing your attention.

Summary

- ✓ Our growing appetite for more of the good life has created work overload.
- ✓ In our hurried world, information is thrown at us at in high volumes. We do not digest it properly and wisdom is often sacrificed in the process. This has created information overload.
- ✓ Using the survey provided, examine your information anxiety symptoms. Look for ways to relieve these symptoms as you read this book.
- ✓ Use the Overload Gauge to help you focus as you develop personalized solutions and periodically monitor your progress.

2 – What Does the Future Hold?

Will The Future Workplace Bring More Life Balance Or More Overload? *Examining economic, social, and technological trends, you will be challenged by the opportunities the future brings. The future offers opportunities for progress and improved effectiveness. More balance and improvement will happen for those who choose to make appropriate changes.*

Complaining is not something I enjoy. I tried to keep my concerns to myself as I observed my husband's deteriorating health and his irritability with me and with the children. I could understand the pressures he was facing and did not want to add to his concerns.

Caring for the children, professional and community activities kept me busy so I had no time for complaining. There was always the hope of a better tomorrow. With every promotion or job change, we hoped that things would improve as routine would be established and work demands would slow down. I was told that in the beginning there would be more work but things would surely get better as time goes by. That was a faint promise, if I ever heard one.

I thought life would get easier when the children got older. That was a dream. Only those who have had teenagers would truly understand why things became harder. With teenage mood swings and a tired, irritable husband, life was going from tough to tougher.

One thing I learned was that life is like a garden patch. Left to its natural state it will always deteriorate. Unless specific actions are taken to make things better, circumstances will always get worse. Based on our experience, the future can get better for those who are committed to choices that bring about balance in life.

During those days I tried to keep my sense of humor and I certainly related to the old woman who after many years of marriage was asked if she ever considered divorce. "Divorce? No," she replied. "Murder? Yes!"

Margaret Habashy, Author

What does the future hold? Will things get better? Will work overload and information overload be a thing of the past? To answer this question we should consider the basic economics of supply and demand for both work and information in the marketplace.

Supply and Demand Economics: Work

As we discussed in Chapter 1, the law of diminishing returns created the need for each of us to work more and more. Our collective demands created the opportunities that helped fuel economic growth. Economic growth provided more work opportunities for those who had to work to fulfill their growing personal expectations.

Further, globalization began to offer poorer nations the products and services once only available to privileged, affluent societies. This continues to increase the demand for the products and services offered in the industrialized world.

Basic economics tell us that there is a strong relationship between **supply and demand** for labor in the marketplace. The year 2000 US census data provides a good indication of labor growth projections over the coming years. It is safe to assume that the US projection represents similar patterns in a majority of the industrialized world. With this in view, **the following table and its related graph** provide us with an interesting picture:

(A) Provides the US population projection for people ages 16 – 64 between the years 2000 and 2035.[3] This population is expected to grow from 178 million in the year 2000 to 213.3 million in 2035.

(B) Uses the year 2000 as a base point representing the demand for work in the marketplace. It also assumes that the economy will grow because of increasing demand and population growth by a compound average of **3%** per year. This is what is called the average GDP (Gross Domestic Product). Now you see that GDP growth results in increased need for more workers from 178 million in the year 2000 to 500.8 million in 2035.

WORKING POPULATION SUPPLY and DEMAND PROJECTIONS			
Year	(A) Population Projection (ages 16-64)	(B) Population Demand = Year 2000 + 3% for GDP Growth	(C) Population Demand Discounted by 50%
2000	178.0	178.0	178.0
2005	188.1	206.3	191.7
2010	196.6	239.2	206.5
2015	200.5	277.3	222.5
2020	202.5	321.4	239.7
2025	203.7	372.6	258.2
2030	206.9	432.0	278.2
2035	213.3	500.8	299.7

(C) Suggests **our hope** for productivity improvement as well as structural changes to the economy. Structural changes will see some work being transferred to parts of the world where there is a greater supply of workers. This is what is often referred to as "outsourcing". Based on this hope we suggest discounting the growth work force demand by 50%. Should this happen, the demand for workers will be less severe. Regretfully, this still leaves us with a significant shortfall.

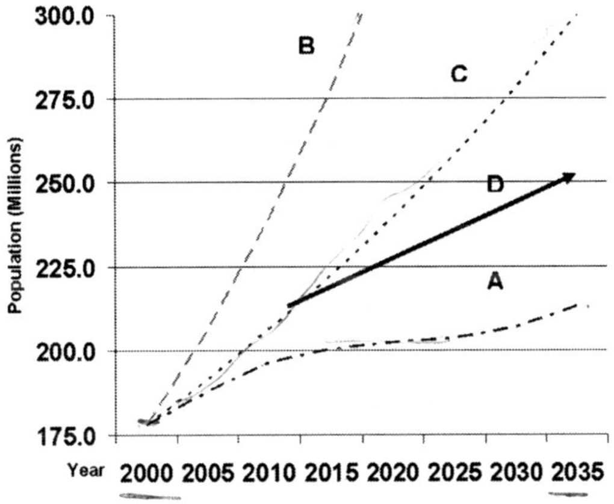

Now you see the delta or gap between the supply (A) and the modified demand (C) for workers in the marketplace. Basic economics tell us that when the demand exceeds the supply, this presents increased pressures on those in the supply line. Granted, those of us in the workplace at that time will be able to ask for more money and get it. However, if you intend to be in the workplace at that time you will be facing an ever-increasing pressure to produce in response to the growing demand that will exist in the marketplace.

This supply and demand problem was confirmed in a July 2002 report by the Organization of Economic Development and

Cooperation, which warned that in the coming years the industrialized world would face a significant shortage of skilled labor.[4] As an example The Financial Post confirmed that a skilled help shortage is hitting Canada. In their December 2002 poll two-thirds of Canadian executives reported that they were having difficulty recruiting skilled labor for their companies.[5]

We added Line (D) to illustrate what we believe is the only solution to this dilemma. We believe that if any of us want to reduce the impact of this crisis of work overload we must raise our value proposition and contribution by:

1. Focusing on higher value roles, goals, and activities
2. Delegating lower value roles, goals, and activities to others who will fill the gap and grow through a proper delegation process.

Attitudes of Young People

Surveys and studies suggest that a significant percentage of young people do not want to work as hard as their parents have. While they want the good life provided by their workaholic parents, they are not willing to pay the price it demands. Many have observed the negative impact that long work hours have had on their parents' health and family life and have decided that it is not worth it. Will that translate into lower demand for products and services? Maybe. One thing for sure, if the coming generation refuses to work the long hours their parents have, the supply of skilled labor will be reduced.

My gauge of success is slowly changing and money is becoming of decreased significance. In my generation there is definitely an overwhelming trend that shares my views. I would far rather be happy and enjoy what I do and make less money as a result of that, than be wealthy and overloaded with work. I'm not opposed to making money; just the opposite, I think it's great, but I'm not willing to sell my life and soul in the pursuit of it. I want work to be a part of my life, not the entirety of it. I want to enjoy my life, all different parts of it. And if the current viewpoints of my generation continue, you may just see a major shift in our culture's life priorities. Then again, maybe you won't!

Noel Habashy, University Admission Counselor

Supply and Demand Economics: Information

As we referenced earlier, technology has made creation, collection, and distribution of information much easier than ever before. The cost of technology is on a constant decline. More and more people have access to communication and information gathering tools. Let us quickly consider the following forms of information input and media.

- **E-mail**: E-mail has become a prevalent tool for personal and corporate communication. Internet cafes and e-mail service rooms are springing up in the most remote parts of the world. The volume of worldwide e-mail has increased by 2000% between 1998 and 2003. This is expected to double over the coming few years.[6]
- **Phone:** With the availability of low cost cell phones and voice over IP, phone subscriptions are exploding. This will multiply meaningful and meaningless chatter on the airwaves. Phone messaging options provide additional communication tools that need to be maintained and serviced frequently.
- **Meetings:** Meetings form a critical part of our information exchange platform. A common complaint among our clients is "We have too many meetings." Studies show that today's managers spend an average of forty percent of their time in meetings. A survey of our clients shows that this amount can go as high as ninety percent.[7] The emerging popularity of video and phone conferencing is creating a new set of challenges.
- **Paper:** Our dream of the paperless office is fast evaporating and the profits of paper mills grow as the demand for paper explodes. "According to David Shenk, author of *Data Smog*, paper consumption per capita in the United States tripled between 1940 and 1980, and tripled again between 1980 and 1990."[8] An article in the National Post in 2001 quoted a study finding that the use of e-mail has increased paper consumption by 40%.[9]

- **Content:** Recent studies by many reputable organizations including University of California at Berkley suggest that the amount of data or content available will double every three to five years.[10] This means that, as a knowledge worker, the amount of information to be processed will continue to increase. This will result in an unprecedented need for mental processing capacity.
- **Always on:** Instant messaging products like IBM SameTime and Instant Messenger from Microsoft are feeding our demands for faster communication exchange. As these products become married to mobile wireless devises and pocket organizers the **"always available", "always on"** expectations will become more of the norm for many in the workplace.

As a futurist, I see two emerging developments that will exasperate the work and information overload problem. The first one is what I call ***"PDAitis"****. The growing use of PDA or Personal Digital Assistance will reduce the latency of our demand expectation to zero. The expectations of time to respond will be reduced significantly, placing more urgency and higher demand on all of us.*

The second factor that gives me concern is the notion of constantly identifiable presence. Emerging technologies will make it possible for people to identify your point of presence at any given time and thus maintain a persistent demand. In a way, you can run but you cannot hide.

Unless we adjust culturally to these factors, I will remain very concerned about what the future holds in relationship to the overload problem.

Dr. Rick Fenton, Strategist, Futurist

So you ask, what does the future hold? If we look at the basic data we can only predict that the future holds more work overload and information overload. But we believe that the future holds a promise of significant change. The future can offer great improvement for you, if you take personal ownership of the overload crisis and make appropriate changes.

As illustrated in line **(D)** of the graph we presented earlier, such changes will help you raise your value contribution by focusing on higher value **roles, goals, and activities**. That is the hope we have and the experience of many of the good people we will introduce throughout this book. This is the objective of the thoughts, tools and tips we will provide in the following chapters.

Technology has had a very positive impact on our lives. Over the coming years I expect we'll see significant advancement in information and communication technologies that will have a considerable impact on connectivity and mobility. From a technological prospective this appears to be very helpful. On the flip side, such advancements will allow us to be accessible 24/7. This will call for better personal mechanisms allowing us to differentiate between work life and personal life. I am sure that most of us have not yet developed these mechanisms.

Today, most of us think of work even when we're not working, whether we are holidaying, walking on a beach on a Saturday morning, or buying groceries. In the future you will not only be tempted by your uncontrolled thoughts, your beach walk will be invaded by those who can reach you through your mobile, interactive device.

Those of us who do not learn now to set personal control mechanisms will be on a slippery slope that will certainly impact negatively on our quality of life.

Ms. Andrea Seymour, Vice President and Chief Information Officer

Summary

- ✓ Economic growth will provide opportunities for work growth that exceed the available supply for talent. Over time, this gap will result in increased workload pressures.
- ✓ We can only bridge the gap between supply and demand by focusing on higher value roles, goals, and activities.
- ✓ Technological advancement and increased information resources could aggravate the information overload problem.

✓ Those who choose to focus on higher value roles, goals, and activities can wisely prioritize reducing their exposure to the causes of overload while at the same time improving the value they contribute to society.

Improvement Indicators

What Indicators Provide Hope For Change? *Emerging social and economic indicators provide hope for positive change. Some of these trends will require painful adjustments. For the most part such adjustments will bring an improved future for those who anticipate them, understand them, and wisely respond to them.*

There are many factors that give us hope for improvement. Let us examine some of them.

- **First:** The overload problem and the need for more life balance are gaining more visibility in the media. Radio and TV personalities are dealing with it more frequently. Healthcare professionals are focusing on this subject and warning us about the negative impacts we face. At the same time politicians are finding it favorable to introduce more family friendly legislation.
- **Second:** As referenced earlier, the younger generation, our children in their teens and twenties, are beginning to rebel against our overworked culture. Having seen the negative impact it has had on their growing years many of them are saying, "I do not want this." While this will reduce the supply of talent in the market place, this may temper our excessive appetite for products and services.
- **Third:** Corporate leaders who traditionally focused on the demand line and ways to grow market share are beginning to see the negative impact work overload is having on the overall productivity. Rational business leaders cannot help but note the growing cost of stress-induced diseases in the workplace.
- **Fourth:** Business leaders are beginning to see the value of encouraging their people to be proactive, bringing ideas that

would make them more effective in what they do. Managers are encouraged to empower people to make choices that help them be more productive. This has opened the door to initiatives such as flex work hours and job sharing. This provides more life balance, as well as improved productivity and effectiveness.

- **Fifth:** Economic restructuring is accelerating the movement of work to markets where the supply for talent is more readily available. In the past, we accepted such migration in certain manufacturing sectors. More of this will be happening among knowledge workers. Some will be threatened as they see professional work migrating to places like India and Eastern Europe. Others will see it as a reason for focusing on higher value roles, goals, and activities.
- **Sixth:** Individuals are taking ownership of the overload problem. This, we believe, is the most important factor. This is the factor that gives us the greatest hope for change. Today more and more individuals realize that making work/life balance a priority is a critical personal choice that demands their attention. Today, we see more individuals making appropriate choices that help them improve effectiveness and reverse the negative impact of work and information overload.

Up until recently money used to be the key motivator for extra work. Today a large percentage of new hires are asking for more life balance as a condition of employment. In their excellent book, *Values Shift*, John B. Izzo, Ph.D., and Pam Withers highlight that a majority of us would rather have more personal time than a pay increase. "When one thousand working adults were asked whether they would rather earn high salaries or earn "enough" doing work that makes the world a better place, 86 percent chose the latter. This is in sharp contrast to a decade or two ago, as confirmed by the results of a survey (previously mentioned in Chapter 2) of graduating MBAs taken ten years apart. The Class of 1989 defined their primary measure of success as power, prestige, and money. The class of 1991 cited successful relationships, a balanced life, and leisure time. Even more recently, respondents responded marriage, health, and ethics!"[11]

Employers need to realize that there is significant gain in helping their employees have interests outside the workplace. By encouraging an environment where employees work to live, not live to work, you will create an atmosphere of trust that leads to higher value from the time spent at work. I believe that having "avocation" leads to energy and success in your vocation. The more you are able to refresh yourself outside the workplace, the more successful you will be in the workplace.

Mr. John McGarry, President and Chief Executive Officer

It is interesting to observe that the cycles of business overload seem to go concurrently with the cycles of personal overload, and this leads me to strongly believe that you cannot isolate business issues from what goes on in an employee's personal life. Employers and managers need to be aware of this fact and must work towards creating a flexible culture where employees are empowered to make choices and take actions.

In our organization we have created a very open and flexible culture - a culture that empowers managers to make their staff more accountable for personal performance. While I have a national HR responsibility in a large organization, I favor a decentralized management style that delegates roles and oversight to regional and functional managers and individual contributors. When you empower people to do what they believe is best, you receive more value in return than if you burden them with too many policies and procedures.

Ms. Grace Cunningham, Manager, Human Resources

As a leader, it is important to me to encourage work life balance because I want working with me individuals whose life priorities go beyond the workplace and reflect sensitivity to the needs of the community and the people around them. Such an individual has the potential of becoming an outstanding leader and has the ability to grow in the business and outside the business world.

Mr. John Ramdeen, Finance Executive, Global Services

Based on our experience with the many clients we served, we firmly believe that motivated individuals empowered to tailor creative solutions in a manner that brings higher value to their corporations and their society can solve the overload problem. As business leaders empower their people to change, individuals will look for ideas and personalized tools that can make them become more effective and gain improved work/life balance.

This is the objective of the **Personal Knowledge Management Framework**.

Personal Knowledge Management Framework

What is the Personal Knowledge Management Framework? *This framework is a solution you can tailor to your own personal needs. We call it a framework because it is made of simple frames representing logical topics. These frames can be modified in response to your particular needs and changing environments.*

The Personal Knowledge Management Framework is a tool to help motivated individuals tailor their own solutions to the work and information overload problem. Illustrated in Diagram 3 this framework is based on our **"Overcoming Work and Information Overload"** workshop.

Why do we call it a framework?

- We call it a framework because it is illustrated in a small collection of frames. Each frame represents a topic that contributes to the solution you create.
- We call it a framework because it is not a rigged system that you must follow or a program that you have to keep. It is a structure that can help you select the frames that are likely to bring you the greatest value at the time when they can be most useful to you.
- We call it a framework because it is a modifiable structure or a set of "Lego" blocks that you can modify to suit your needs.

When our son was small he loved "Lego". He enjoyed the packaging and the success of building what the company illustrated but his greatest sense of achievement came when he created his own design. Please consider the **Personal Knowledge Management Framework** as your own set of "Lego" blocks. We will provide you with many thoughts and tips that will help you get started. Use the templates that we offer to move faster in developing and building your own solution. Do not hesitate to modify and tailor our thoughts, tips and templates to fit your particular need.

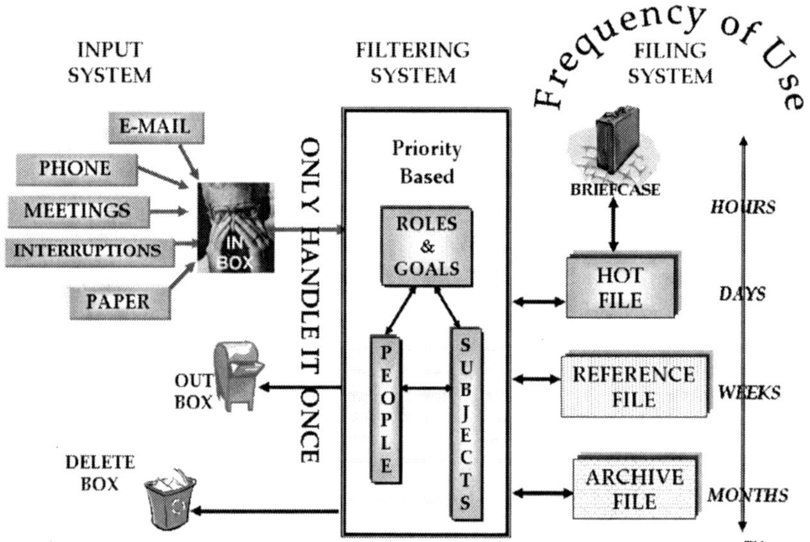

Diagram 3: Personal Knowledge Management Framework™

You may notice in Diagram 3 that the framework is made of three sections:

- **Section One is the Filtering system.** We have relied on ageless wisdom to provide common sense principles to help you filter wisely.
- **Section Two is the Input system.** Here we have provided practical thoughts and tips to help you manage the floodgates of information and demands placed on your life.
- **Section Three is the Filing system.** Information is valuable only when we can apply it to the outside world in a timely

and proper manner. This filing structure will help you reduce information clutter and file information so you can find it when you need it. This easy to use filing system is based on a long established approach used by successful libraries world wide.

Summary

- ✓ The Personal Knowledge Management Framework is not a system or a program; it is a tool to be tailored by and fitted to personal use.
- ✓ The Personal Knowledge Management Framework is made of simple frames representing individual topics in three groups:
  - o The Filtering System provides commonsense principles to help you filter wisely.
  - o The Input System provides thoughts or tips to help you manage the sources of overload.
  - o The Filing System provides a filing system to reduce information clutter and help you find what you need when you need it.

PART TWO:

FILTERING - KEEPING OVERLOAD AT BAY

- Filtering on High Value Roles
  - **Playing Your Roles on Different Stages**
- Filtering on High Value Goals
- Filtering on High Value Relationships
- Filtering on High Value Subjects
  - **Important And Urgent – Defining the Difference**
- Have a Mission Statement

Part Two – Filtering - Keeping Overload at Bay

Can Filtering Help You? *The challenge most of us face is not in choosing between the good and the bad. The challenge is filtering, to choose between the good and the best. Developing your own filtering system will help you focus, prioritize, and choose what is the best.*

Most of us develop bad habits not because we desire them, but because we do not have enough motivation to break them or avoid them. We would change our bad habits if we had sufficient rewards from changing them, or if we were faced with the negative consequences of our bad habits. As human beings, we are subject to the law of "the carrot and the stick".

The motivation to change our overloaded world must come from within each of us. As we think of the ever-looming demand of our growing economy and the increased pressure this will bring, we hope that fear may motivate some of us. As we think of the immense future growth potential, we hope that all of us are challenged by the opportunity we have to bring higher value to society and to those who are important to us. Those of us who accept this challenge will reap great personal rewards and benefits.

In other words, each of us must develop our own motivation based on an honest understanding of the high price we are likely to pay for our overloaded lives if we do not change, and the potential rewards we are likely to gain, if we do change.

From an old workaholic I say to all workaholics, young and old, learn to prioritize and filter out what is not important. This is the most important thing you can do for yourself and for those for whom you care. If you do not, you may wake up one day and find that the price you have paid is way too high. And then it is often too late to renegotiate. Believe me, I speak from experience.

Ms. Nada Pavic, Business Development Manager

The priority based filtering system is a strategic tool that provides a thinking process. We believe that given the opportunity to think carefully, most of us will be motivated to change for the better. Based on our clients' experiences, as you use this thinking tool, you will develop your own filtering system that will help you **focus on higher value roles, goals, and activities**.

Diagram 4 illustrates the priority based filtering system as a dynamic interrelationship of three critical areas:

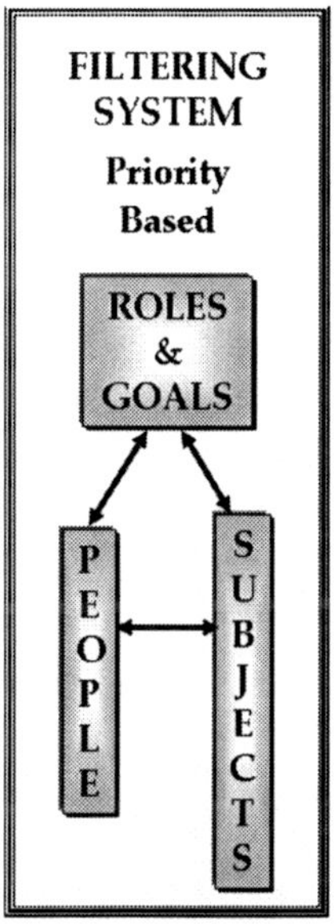

Diagram 4

1. **Roles and Goals:** Your roles and their related goals are the primary driving force in this filter. Roles are different from job titles and are seldom defined in job descriptions. In our hurried and busy lives we seldom take time to define the roles we play on the stage of life. We decide and act without regularly examining our actions in relationship to our critical goals. This can change as you define your high value roles relating them to high value goals and use this to help you filter the information you receive and the demands placed on your life.
2. **People:** As a knowledge worker, people are your information exchange partners. The people in your sphere of life are the target and recipients of your value proposition. As you think of people you must include yourself as one of the most important people. Your personal well-being and the information you need for your growth and development are the vehicles by which you provide and increase the value you bring to others in the world around you.

   Some may suggest that to think of value as it relates only to people is rather narrow and selfish. While this may be true, we must realize that all things were created to add value to mankind, as mankind assumes the caretaker role for all things created.
3. **Subjects:** The information subjects that you seek and

collect are a support infrastructure to help you play your role and achieve your goals and deliver high value to the people around you. In our information-cluttered world we must stop and ask, "How does this information help me relate to my roles and goals and how will this information benefit my interaction with my important people?"

In general, people never admit that they are overloaded. The first step to overcoming overload is to accept the reality of overload. The second step is to be willing to make personal change within the business culture you are working in. Once you have made the commitment to change your causes of overload, it is important to communicate your desired plan to the various levels in the organization in a manner that is appropriate to each person.

In our organization we have created what I call a listening culture. In such a culture, the employees have the freedom to discuss issues openly, share constructive feedback and advice. If you are overloaded, it is important to share how you feel with someone who can listen to you and support you in making appropriate changes. A peer or a caring manager can be a vital resource in times of stress or overload.

Ms. Grace Cunningham, Manager, Human Resources

Information and work overload is a common, and for many of us, a constant problem in the workplace today. This is a reality that I had to face. My first step in fighting my overload problem was to acknowledge that it was a personal problem that I had to solve myself. I also had to admit that if I did not conquer the problem that it would have a seriously detrimental impact on my life. Only then could I make the mental shift and take personal responsibility for fixing the overload problem.

The second step was to realize that as it was a significant problem the solution would not be reached with a simple set of techniques and tools. Rather, this problem required an integrated solution. While techniques and tools were helpful, for me the real breakthrough came from changing my attitudes, and in clarifying my roles and goals.

Mr. Doug Stirling, Director of Corporate Accounting

Over the years I learned that it is very important to set realistic expectations of others and myself. As a leader there will always be more to do than you are able to do. It is very easy to fall victim to unrealistic self-imposed expectations. There is always more that you wish you could control than you really do control. You must learn to say no, so that you can say, "Yes" to the truly important priorities. Another important lesson I learned is that you cannot be responsible for things over which you have no control. It sounds simple, but so often we get caught up in to trying to manage things that are really not ours to manage or we are held accountable for results in areas over which we have no control. Both approaches lead to stress! As a result you cannot assume responsibility for what you do not control. Accepting such reality has had a great impact on my work life balance.

Ms. Karen MacDonald, Regional Director, Quality Improvement and Education

Summary

- ✓ We indulge in bad habits when we lack the motivation to focus on what is best.
- ✓ To overcome the overload problem we must individually be motivated by the potential of adding higher value and consider the risks associated with the negative impact of work and information overload.
- ✓ You can filter wisely by relating your high value roles and goals to the people who are your information exchange partners, as well as the subject matter and the information you collect and need to support your roles.

Please note: This section will be of particular value to those who had a high score in the Statements 1 to 7 of the Overload Gauge in Chapter 1.

3 – Filtering on High Value Roles

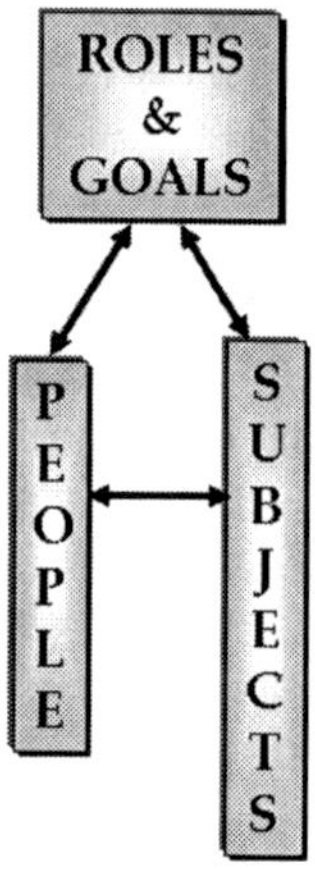

How Do You Describe Your High Value Roles? *Back in the 1600's, Shakespeare told us that all the world is a stage and each of us have many parts to play on it. We each have our entrance and exits and each in our time play many parts. On the stage of life the roles you play are more important than the titles you hold. We challenge you to filter by focusing on the highest value roles.*

Shakespeare"[12] provided us with powerful imagery that we hope you will keep in mind as we challenge you to **filter on high value roles.**

Suppose you meet a stranger at a party. As the conversation develops you indicate that you work for XYZ Company. He proceeds to ask you, "What role do you play at XYZ Company?" What would you say? Do you have a clear answer that communicates the high value you bring to your work environment?

Most of us when asked such a question quickly provide our title. If the questioner persists, we respond highlighting our functional or organizational responsibilities or work habits. It is easy for us to define our roles based on what we do. We forget that we are not called human doings, but we are called human **BEINGS** because our roles are best defined by what we are expected to **BE**, not merely by what we are expected to **DO**.

While some titles imply certain roles they seldom define the high value roles that we need to aspire to deliver. History books are filled with individuals who had impressive titles but their lives were void of valuable contributions to the people around them. At the same time many walked this planet with humble titles fulfilling great roles and influenced many lives for good.

Titles and organizational structure come with their own baggage and implied values that are often misleading. Titles often bring certain expectations of priorities that are not realistic or may even drive you to compromised priorities. Titles cause you to act based on legacy assumptions and expectations that are ill defined or poorly communicated.

If "All the world's a stage," then on this universal platform, we all have the same title. We are all actors. Our success on the stage of life is not based on our title. Our value is directly related to our ability to play our high value roles, be supported by and provide the needed support for others who share the stage with us. It is critical that we pay utmost attention to what we are expected to **BE** as we enter and exit.

Recently, I was speaking with a Deputy Minister of Health about the mistake we often make of placing people in leadership roles based on their business or clinical skills without giving enough attention to their social and caring qualities. A person's knowledge or competencies do not necessarily ensure that he or she is a good fit for the roles assigned in an organization.

Mr. John McGarry, President and Chief Executive Officer

On the various stages of life you need to take an active part in defining your roles. If you do not exercise that ability, others will assume roles for you. They will assume roles that reflect their own priorities. They will impose definitions that are biased by their own expectations, not necessarily by your abilities and limitations. They will impose role descriptions that may be in conflict with your values. Being active in defining your role involves honest communication and negotiation with those who share the various stages of life with you.

Our experience as husband and wife highlights the importance of negotiating and re-evaluating personal and business roles. We have been married for over thirty-one years. As a newly married couple, we were highly committed to having the best relationship possible. Having come from different cultural backgrounds, our expectations of each other's roles were significantly different. Our assumptions were gravely faulty. It was not until a major crisis occurred in our relationship that we realized the importance of defining our roles as husband and wife. Until then we had stressful conceptions of what we were expected to **BE**.

When we became parents, these roles as husband and wife had to be re-examined and modified. Again, when we became business partners in Integrity+ Consulting we had to re-negotiate our roles; as husband and wife, we were committed to bringing the highest value possible to our new clients. We needed to find ways to complement each other as business partners.

Since our work requires extensive research and client communications we agreed that Margaret's primary role is to be "the brain" of our partnership. She feels comfortable with this role and it fits her temperament and love for research. On the other hand, Baha acts as "the mouthpiece" for our communication needs. He is good at this and it suits his sanguine personality. As we realigned our roles we both feel fulfilled and our clients appreciate the high value they receive from our workshops.

As I grew older I learned that I couldn't be all things to all people. Learning to negotiate for realistic expectations is a vital skill that will help you avoid becoming a victim of an overloaded life.

Ms. Pat Clinch, Director Organizational Development

Your world is a multi-faceted stage. As you face each day you have unlimited opportunities to play many roles on a variety of stages. Before you get involved in any role, you must answer some critical questions:

1. Do you support the values of the drama that is being performed on that stage?
2. Can you and the key participants in the drama engage in open communication regarding your role and that of others on the stage?
3. How do you define your role?

Assuming that your answers to questions 1 and 2 are positive, then the next critical step is to define what are you expected to **BE**. One of the simplest ways in defining what you are expected to be is to agree on the most important **adjectives** that describe each role.

As we are called **"human beings"** our success on the stage is highly dependent on the ability to embody the character we are to **BE**. Our success is directly related to our ability to communicate the attitudes and the value of the person we are expected to **BE**. Our effectiveness is impacted more by the soft skills we are expected to demonstrate than by our knowledge or competencies.

Until recently, hiring practices were heavily based on a person's academic and business achievements. We often assumed that if the person held degrees in a specific field, he or she would do well in certain roles that require assumed knowledge or competencies. We wrongly expected a person with similar titles in other places to be capable of handling similar profiles. Today behaviour-based interviewing and examining character references are more important than the resume a candidate may present. It is critical that we ensure the proper fit of the candidate on the new stage he or she is expected to perform.

In the business world, whether you are a senior leader or junior manager, priority based filtering is a key success factor. Having roles that are clearly aligned to corporate objectives is vital to personal and business effectiveness. One of the key roles of a leader is to rely on experience and filter away urgency from his people. This will help them focus on what is important and not be distracted by urgent demands. When talking to overloaded people I often find that as much as half of what they are doing is working on the wrong thing or spending too much time on things that do not deserve so much time and should be put aside.

Mr. Jim Wright, Operation Executive

Exercise

In the following **Template A**:

1. List the five most important roles you play in your place of work and then list the most important attributes or adjectives that describe each role. As an example, if you were to choose the role of a **coach,** your adjectives may be knowledgeable, committed, empathetic, disciplined, fair, helpful, available ...

Note: Avoid **"title imposed roles".** Roles that are familiar to your job environment bring along with them past opinions, assumptions, and expectations that are often misleading and burdensome. For example, supposing you hold the title **"manager"** you will find that you will fall victim to others' assumptions, expectations and biases. By moving away from "title imposed roles" you can redefine your title by breaking it down into more definable roles such as **coach, model, helper, overseer, watchdog** etc. This will help you decide which of these delivers highest value and is deserving of your focus. To help your thinking process, the following lists examples of roles and adjectives or attributes that you may consider:

Example of Roles

- o Advisor
- o Advocate
- o Arbitrator
- o Catalyst
- o Champion
- o Coach
- o Confidant
- o Creator
- o Enabler
- o Encourager
- o Facilitator
- o Influencer
- o Listener
- o Mentor
- o Model
- o Motivator
- o Observer
- o Organizer
- o Overseer
- o Participant
- o Partner
- o Provider
- o Resource
- o Shepherd
- o Sounding board
- o Substitute
- o Supporter
- o Watchdog

Example of Attributes or Adjectives

- o Adaptable
- o Affirming
- o Aggressive
- o Analytical
- o Articulate
- o Calm
- o Charismatic
- o Clear
- o Committed
- o Compassionate
- o Competitive
- o Conscientious
- o Creative
- o Decisive
- o Demanding
- o Dependable
- o Determined
- o Diplomatic
- o Direct
- o Disciplined
- o Encouraging
- o Ethical
- o Experienced
- o Fair
- o Generous
- o Helpful
- o Honest
- o Independent
- o Knowledgeable
- o Loyal
- o Perceptive
- o Persevering
- o Persuasive
- o Practical
- o Provocative
- o Realistic
- o Supportive
- o Understanding
- o Wise

Template A: Roles Inventory

List Important Roles	List the most important adjectives to describe how you see each role.
Ex: Person	*Alive, Active, Wise, Growing, Involved*

Choose five important people who share the stage with you. Ask them, using a similar template, to list the five most important roles you are expected to play and list the most important adjectives to describe each role.

2. Compare your answers. Discuss the differing opinions and negotiate for appropriate compromises.
3. Write any appropriate changes you need to make in fulfilling your role.

Please note: If this is the first time you are doing such an exercise, you may find this awkward in the beginning. **Do not let this hold you back. Remember your goal is progress, not perfection.** Later on this will become second nature to you.

It is very easy to let professional roles overtake personal life. Recently, I stepped back and examined my roles as a young mother, wife and manager. I quickly realized that children, by virtue of their dependence, seem to take priority in my personal life. This, coupled with professional demands, made it easy to overlook the needs of my spouse who seemed independent and self-sufficient. Now I am paying more attention to my role as a wife and the critical importance of developing my relationship with my spouse.

Ms. Donna Johnston, People Manager

Summary

- ✓ Defining your roles is one of the most critical steps in developing your filtering system.
- ✓ If you do not participate in defining your roles, others will assume them for you.
- ✓ A simple approach in defining your roles is to list your most important roles, using Template A, along with the most important adjectives that describe each role.
- ✓ Compare how you describe these roles with the description of others who share the same stage with you.
- ✓ Negotiate appropriate compromises, where needed.

Performing Your Roles on Multiple Stages

What Kind Of Stage Suits You Best? *Life presents each of us with three stages on which we play our roles and demonstrate our value proposition. They are: The Leadership Stage, The Project Stage, and The Operational Stage. To a great extent, the stage impacts the roles you play. Your effectiveness is directly related to your ability to choose your primary stage and your flexibility in moving from one stage to the other as the need arises.*

We all play different roles at differing times in our lives. Such roles require us to portray different characters and perform different tasks on a variety of stages. The stage on which you feel most fulfilled is the one that provides you with the ability to **BE** what you like to be and **DO** what you like to do. Very often it is on this stage that you are likely to deliver your highest value.

We suggest that we all operate on three stages at different times. Diagram 5 illustrates these three interdependent stages.

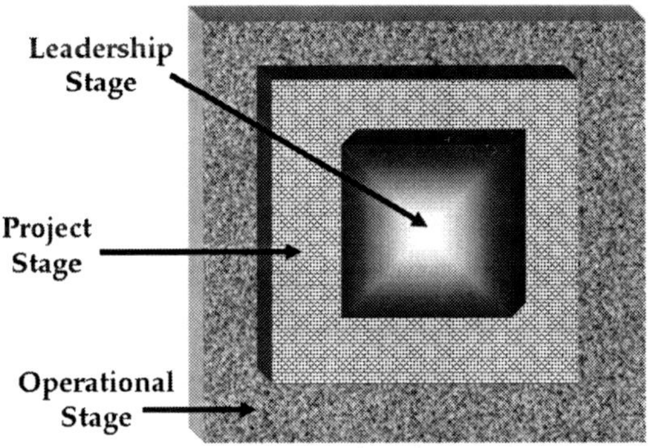

Diagram 5: Multiple Stages

While we all must play on all three stages we are likely to be most comfortable with one specific stage. Ensuring that your primary role affords you the opportunity to be on such a stage is critical to your fulfillment and your success. At the same time, your effectiveness is highly related to your flexibility and your ability to move from one stage to the other when needed. Let us briefly examine the differing stages.

The Leadership Stage: The leadership stage is the place where you exercise leadership skills playing the role of coach, influencer, guide, visionary, and entrepreneur. On the leadership stage your value is most likely related to how the people around you perceive you and respond to you. On the leadership stage you call people to positive change that enhances their value contributions. On the leadership stage the primary beneficiaries of your role are those you lead. In the process you are likely to receive tangible and non-tangible rewards for your influence. We realize that, in one way or another, at least for some of the time, we are all called to be leaders. We lead people by our words but even more importantly, by our example.

The Project Stage, The project stage is the place where you leverage your changing world and the people around you. Some of the roles you play on the project stage include that of:

- A resource who contributes knowledge, competencies or experience to the project team
- An advisor who provides answers to critical questions
- A Project Authority who is able to arbitrate conflicting priorities and ensure the availability of needed funds and resources
- A champion who is able to rally for the support of, or to sell new ideas needed for project success
- A planner who has the skills needed to articulate realistic tasks and milestones
- A manager who ensures the proper execution of needed tasks at the appropriate time

Delivering maximum value on the project stage is directly impacted by your ability to negotiate the role that best suits you on a project team. The world around us is changing very fast. Projects by nature leverage and add value through managing change. Projects have a unique advantage of providing measurable progress towards an expected target.

In our consulting practice we often liken projects to having a baby. They have a beginning and an end. Projects require the participation of committed individuals with clearly defined roles. While some project tasks are painful, in the end there are visible positive changes and benefits that call for celebration.

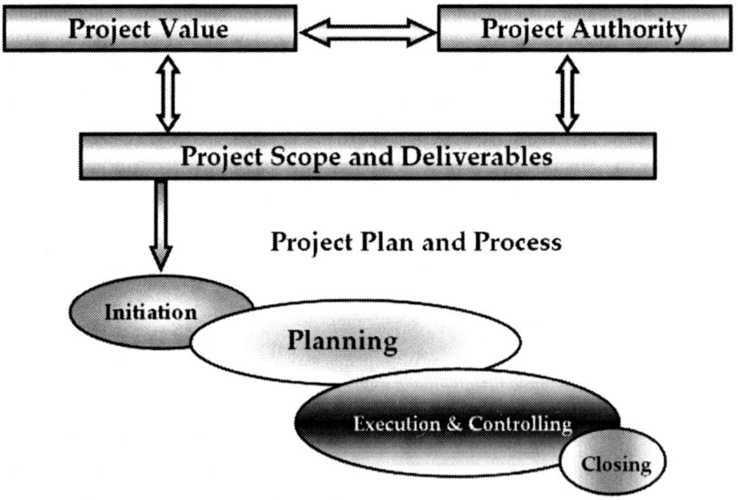

Diagram 6: Project Success Factors

Your ability to fulfill such a role on the project stage depends on the presence of what we call **"the key project success factors".** Illustrated in Diagram 6 these factors include:

- **High project value:** Too many projects are started without clearly articulated benefit statements. A benefit statement responds to one simple question, **"Why should we do this?"** Benefit statements clearly define the expected changes and outcome of a project. Benefit statements reflect the tangible and non-tangible benefits that will result from investing efforts and resources in the stated project. Benefit statements serve to mobilize and recruit appropriate players and project participants.
- **Responsible Project Authority:** The Project Authority is the person who has the responsibility of funding the project. Very often it is the person who has the vision to see the high level benefits of the project or who is most likely to receive most of the project benefits.
- **Project Scope and Deliverables:** Regretfully, far too often we see clients starting a project without a clear definition or

agreement on scope. A clearly articulated scope should highlight what is included and what is excluded from the project considerations. A list of key deliverables must be documented and have the approval of the Project Authority. Any changes to the project scope must be well controlled.

- **Reasonable project plan:** A project plan is a clear list of projected tasks. Such a plan defines the interrelationship between the project players. It provides reasonable estimates of costs and efforts that can be measured against the expected benefits. It sets the stage for rational expectations and timelines. It helps in avoiding disappointments and frustrations. The project plan has multiple, often overlaying, phases that include initiation, planning, execution /controlling and closing/celebration.

Identifying your comfortable roles on a well-structured, high value, projects stage will help you add significant value to your ever changing world..

The Operational Stage: Unlike the project stage, which leverages change, the operational stage leverages consistency and predictability. It is on this stage that we expect smooth operational production. Here you come to expect maximum output for minimum time and energy investment. It is like keeping the engine oiled or the gas tank filled. The operational stage is the place where risks are minimized through predictable outcomes. On the operational stage you play the role of an operator, a controller, an administrator or a watchdog…

Regretfully, as a result of the changing world the operational serenity is often invaded by problems. Just as we likened the project stage to having babies, the operational stage is like raising children. Some of us are better suited for this stage than others but all of us have some elements of involvement at some point in our lives.

Some episodes on the operational stage are stressful or unpleasant. Some of us on the operational stage feel that our primary role is fighting fires, fixing mistakes or what we often call "changing diapers". Yes, that is correct; changing a baby's diapers is not a pleasant phase of parenthood. Sometimes in our business world we spend far too much time "changing diapers".

Let us give you a simple analogy. When our children were little I considered diaper changing tasks to be the most unpleasant. If it were not for the flexibility and wisdom of a good mother, our children would have been in diapers for a very long time. Moving these operational problems of "diaper changes" into a "toilet training project" required leadership, foresight, and commitment. The toilet training project adhered to specific disciplines and required ongoing support. During the project you saw incremental progress. In the end there was a major celebration for all project participants. Ultimately the benefits definitely outweighed the investments and the non-tangible costs.

Remember this analogy if your operational world is filled with "diaper changing" episodes. Take time to exercise leadership. Move the issues to the project stage. Define the value, define the scope, ensure the availability of a credible Project Authority, document a rational toilet training plan, execute your plan with the support of a good team, and celebrate the resulting benefits!

Baha Habashy

Summary

- ✓ We all play roles on three differing yet often interrelated stages. They are: the leadership stage, the project stage, and the operational stage.
- ✓ Each of these three stages offers different values and is suitable for different individuals and roles.
- ✓ We each have a primary stage on which we feel most comfortable and fulfilled. At all times we need to exercise wisdom and flexibility to play on stages other than our primary stage in response to our changing world.
- ✓ If problems persist on the operational stage it is time to exercise leadership by initiating appropriate projects to fix the problem.

4 – Filtering on High Value Goals

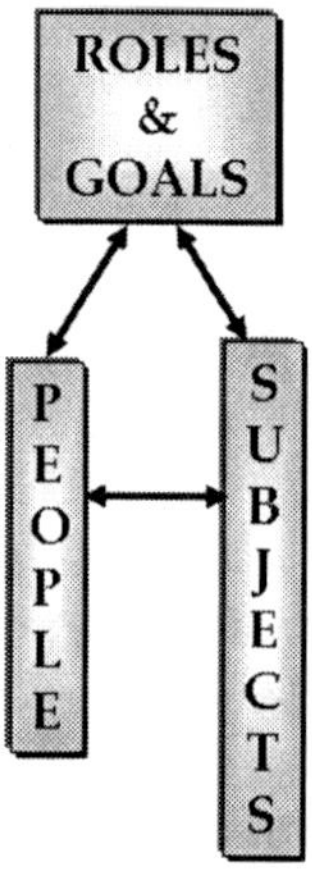

What Are the SMART Goals That Direct Your Life Priorities? *Goals energize you and direct your progress. Once you define your high value roles it is critical that you articulate specific goals that help you prioritize your activities and track your progress.*

While your roles define what you are expected to **BE,** your goals define what you are expected to **DO.** Living without goals leads to an aimless life. The old saying is true "If you aim at nothing, you will surely get there." Accepting a role without defining what you are expected to do could lead to unrealistic expectations of yourself and others. This often results in disappointments and overloaded lives. Unless you actively participate in developing your goals, others will assume them for you.

Someone has suggested that we all have goals. Some are clear goals; others are fuzzy goals. Some are good goals and some are foolish goals. Here we want to discuss the importance of smart goals. **SMART** provides the acronyms for **S**pecific, **M**easurable, **A**greed upon, **R**ealistic and **T**ime dependent.

Specific: Goals need to be specific. In sport a goal is a very clearly marked point. We suggest that a specific goal is one that can be verified by one of the five senses or can be confirmed by scientific measurements. If you were to say that your goal is to be a good coach, then this is subjective and open to interpretation. It is highly based on the image you and others have of what a good coach is like. But if you were to say that you want to coach five people in e-mail etiquette, then you have a more specific goal. Specific goals are smart goals because they communicate value that justifies the discipline and effort required to achieve them.

Measurable: Having a measurable goal allows you to gauge your progress towards reaching it. So if you were to say that your goal is to find five people to coach, then you can measure your progress as you find the first, second, third, fourth, and fifth person. Measuring progress is a very critical self-motivator. Measurable goals are smart goals because they help you make appropriate and timely changes to your action plans when necessary.

Agreed upon: Before you embark on any goal you must be sure that your goal is agreed upon by all those have an important stake in it. Unless you and the five individuals you have targeted for your coaching role agree on their need for your coaching, you have no chance of achieving your goal. In other words, agreed upon goals are smart goals because they are backed by the support of other people who are committed to the same outcome.

Realistic: A common mistake encountered by most of us is that we underestimate the effort and the investment required by most goals. One thing that has helped us very much is to "aim high and goal low". It is good to set high and lofty visions but it is wise to set realistic goals. Setting realistic goals that can be easily achieved will encourage you as you progress to higher value goals and activities.

Time dependent: Like any drama on a stage a smart goal has a starting and a finishing point. Goals with endless timelines lead to frustration and apathy. Your smart goal should read "to coach the five members of my operational team in e-mail etiquette for thirty days, starting today." Time dependent goals are smart goals because they help you avoid the natural temptation to procrastinate.

Now it is important to note that no goal is 100% assured. Smart goals are a statement of faith - faith that is compelling and reasonable. We live in an imperfect, often uncertain world. Very often fear of failure holds us back from setting goals. Do not let your desire for perfection and risk aversion restrain you from determining goals. If need be, list appropriate assumptions associated with your goal. Remember, goals are outward expressions of your roles. If you do not set them clearly, others will assume them for you.

I am still working on improving my work life balance. This is not easy with the high demands of the sales world. But I have learned to be more diligent in clarifying my priorities and managing people's expectations of me. You can never please everyone. If you spread yourself too thin, you will please no one.

We live in a culture where we are often valued based on what we do. My advice to the overloaded person is to be brutally honest with yourself and clearly define what is important to you. At the end of the day there are very few things that significantly impact our life. Prioritize aggressively and reprioritize if necessary; this will allow you to keep your commitments. People will respect you more when they know where you stand.

Ms. Susan Malenica, Regional Director, Business Development

Exercise

1. Consider one of your most important roles. It could be one of the roles you listed in the exercise in the previous template; for example, it could be the role of a **coach.**
2. Using the following Template B that follows at the end of this chapter, define two SMART goals associated with this role. For each goal write the **accomplishment** you want to see happen.
3. List the **actions** you need to undertake towards reaching this goal. Start every action statement using a **verb**. Note that for each accomplishment you may have more than one related action or activity.
4. Indicate the target completion action date for this action.

Please note: If this is the first time you are doing such an exercise, you may find this awkward in the beginning. **Do not let this hold you back. Remember your goal is progress, not perfection.** Later on this will become second nature to you.

Summary

- ✓ Your high value roles must have meaningful outcomes associated with them.
- ✓ If you do not participate in defining your goals, others will assume them for you.
- ✓ **SMART** goals are **S**pecific, **M**easurable, **A**greed upon, **R**ealistic and **T**ime dependent.
- ✓ **SMART** goals are the best way to define what you are expected to **DO** on the various stages of life.
- ✓ Goals are a statement of faith based on your best understanding of beliefs and estimates.
- ✓ Define your goals using Template B by writing what you want to see happen as an accomplishment. Then list the actions you need to take towards achieving your accomplishment along with the target completion date.

Template B-Goals Inventory

Role	SMART Goal – What? What do I want to happen? (Accomplishment)	How? How will I know it happened? (Actions)	By When? Target date
Ex: Person	*Improve health by losing five pounds*	*Get medical check*	*Jan 20*
		Exercise 60 minutes 6 days a week	*Feb - June*
		No snacks mid day	*Feb - July*

5 – Filtering on High Value Relationships

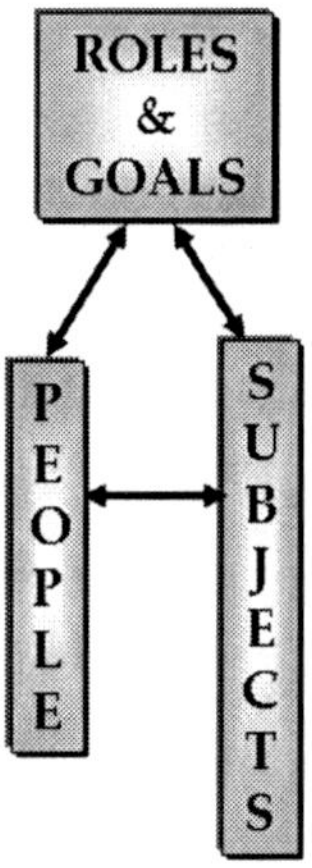

Who Are Your Important And Teachable People? *People are your information exchange partners. Your value proposition is directly related to the positive impact you have on the people touched by your roles and influenced by your goals. Here you are encouraged to identify your important people, your teachable people, and your draining people.*

As knowledge workers, most of us add value by impacting the lives of other human beings for good. Even those of us who care for animals and natural resources must admit that the final link of what we do is often related to the well-being of humankind. Every one of us who knows how to do good and neglects to do so, is short-changing his fellowman of the best we can offer. With this in view, we must always inventory our relationships and assess our ability to impact the lives of others for good.

We have been taught that all people are equal. Yes, all people are equal under the law, all people are equal in the Day of Judgment, and all people are equal when it comes to death and taxes. But not all people are equally important when it comes to prioritizing our personal and business relationships. Our time, energy, and resources are finite and we need to invest them where we can deliver the highest value and where we have the maximum impact.

Important, Teachable, and Draining People

In his thought-provoking book, *Restoring Your Spiritual Passion,* Gordon MacDonald suggests that in our lives we have different types of people.[13] We recommend reading his book along with Stephen Covey and his bestseller, *The Seven Habits of Highly Effective People.*[14] Here we provide you with an illustration that could help you filter life demands based on the impact you have on people and the impact people have on you.

Diagram 7 illustrates three circles based on the impact of three different people groups. They are:

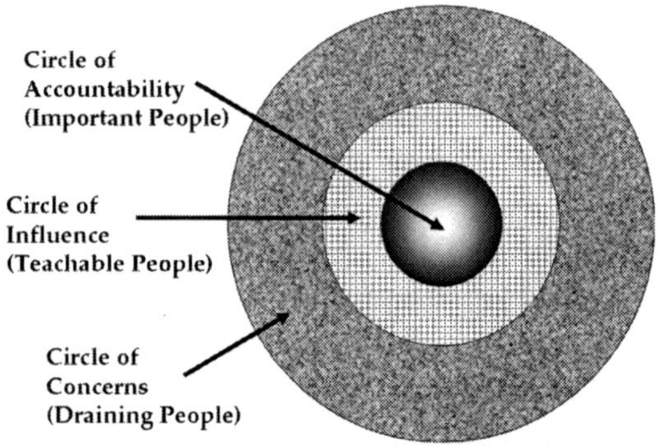

Diagram 7: Circles of Relationships

- The circle of accountability holding your Important People
- The circle of influence which holds the Teachable People
- The circle of concerns which holds your Draining People

1. **The circle of accountability:** While all human beings are important not all of them should have the same priority in our attention or focus. Her we recommend that you consider the important people as **the people who help you define your roles and the people who are critical to the achievement of your goals**.

On the stage of life the **people who help you define your roles** are important people because they appreciate and understand the roles you need to play. They are individuals with whom you have a strong, open relationship that allows them to provide input into your values and character. They are people who are committed to your success and/or whose success is highly dependent on your success. In many cases they are individuals to whom you are accountable or those you ask to hold you accountable. The important people may include special family members, key people in your business organization and others you consider mentors or great influencers on your values and thoughts.

We should hasten to say that some of the important people who have helped us define our roles are writers. Through their writings and ageless wisdom they have impacted many for good.

The people who help you define your roles may be different for each role. But at all times keep that number to a mere handful; otherwise you may be faced with the confusing task of prioritizing conflicting opinions.

Also, the **important people are those who are critical to the achievement of your goals**. SMART, high value goals are often achieved through interdependent relationships with others. Such people often, directly or indirectly, derive benefit from your success. These people may include your children, colleagues, key customers, and/or suppliers of the products and services you need.

Once again, you will find that as you grow in your value contribution you will need to prioritize and reduce the number of people who are critical to the achievement of your goals. If you do not do this, you run the risk of diluting your impact and relationships.

As you take inventory of your important people, do not overlook counting yourself in that list. Your values, character and attributes are the most critical factors in helping you define your roles. Your health, talents and abilities are most important assets in helping you achieve your goals.

2. **The circle of influence:** This circle holds the teachable people who are influenced by your character and/or your attitudes. They admire your behavior and your life values. They consider you a model in certain aspects of your life and wish to learn from you. Teachable people are in your circle of influence by their choice and your invitation. With them you have a mentoring, coaching or leadership relationship.

The teachable people are committed to you and you invest time and interest in them, as you help them grow. You seldom expect tangible or monetary rewards from your teachable people. However, as they grow you are energized and rewarded by seeing them progress and do well. Sometimes your teachable people are the people to whom you can delegate some of your roles and responsibilities as you move on to higher value roles, goals, and activities.

Let us see how this works. Suppose you realize that you are on too many committees and you want to free more time for your family. You approach one of your teachable people who can benefit from the experience of being on that committee and help him or her decide to take your role. As you do this you move to a new role in his or her life. You may become a coach or an encourager. As you watch him or her fulfill a new role you are satisfied and fulfilled by such progress. At the same time you are freed to pursue higher value roles, goals, and activities.

Your teachable people are the legacy of a life on life investment - the legacy you leave as you move on life's journey. Your teachable people are the ones who will most likely have the fondest and best memories of the impact you have had on their life.

3. **The circle of concerns:** This circle holds the draining people. These are the people who do not fit in the first two categories. People concerns are the most draining of life experiences.
    - Draining people are individuals whose behaviors and attitudes bring you concern and over tax your emotional well-being while resulting in little improvement on their part.
    - Draining people repeatedly face the same problems, complain about the same issues but seldom take action to change eventual outcomes.
    - Draining people are often critical of others, disruptive in meetings and seldom proactive in facing life challenges.
    - Draining people often deal with superficial symptoms and are seldom ready to confront the causes of problems.
    - Draining people enter our lives in a variety of forms. They come in the form of individuals as well as in the form of negative media reports, editorials, or TV programs that promote violence and negative behavior or lifestyles.

As a Christian minister, the model of Jesus Christ impresses me and I try to follow His example. He prioritized His life around people. He knew His important people and focused on them. He spent much time praying and talking with God and that helped Him define his important roles. At the same time, he focused on those who needed his teaching and healing ministry, as they were critical to the achievement of his goals.

Early in His ministry He identified twelve teachable people and focused on them. And within that group he identified Peter, James and John in whom he invested extra effort and time. These few carried his legacy of impacting the world for good.

Rev. Ernest LaFont, Pastor and Police Chaplain

To me, the important people are not limited to those in authority over me. Important people are those that help shape my roles and are interested in my personal development. Important people include my dear wife, because of her commitment to me, and to a differing degree other family members and friends because of the positive influence they have on my life.

On the opposite side, draining people often have a negative impact on the achievement of my goals and on how I feel about the roles that I undertake.

It is important to filter out draining people in order to avoid their negative impact. The first step I took in filtering out draining people was to identify them based on their negative effect. The next step was to limit my exposure to them by making our encounters more structured and controlled. Finally as I realized that in filtering out these people in this way I also risked losing potential positive benefits such an individual may bring to my own goals or development so I have tended to re-evaluate this labeling often.

Mr. Doug Stirling, Director of Corporate Accounting

Regretfully, most leaders spend far too much time with the draining people; they seldom clearly identify their teachable people and take the important people for granted.

Margaret Habashy, Author

A question we are often asked is, ***"Can important people be draining people as well?" The answer is yes.*** *To illustrate, let me share with you three experiences:*

My Precious Girl:

Like any father my firstborn, Rebecca, was the apple of my eye. Rebecca was very critical to the achievement of the goals I set as she called me Daddy. Many parents will relate to the sudden change that happened when my precious girl became a teenager. My very important person became one of my most draining people. She told me that she did not need parents anymore.

Fearful and anxious, I struggled with this sudden change. While she became one of my draining people I could not abandon my role as her parent. What I had to do was limit my exposure to her destructive moods swings, avoid confrontations, and find common grounds for reasonable communication.

Today, Rebecca is in her twenties. While still her parent, my goals and relationship has evolved. Rebecca has become one of my most delightful, teachable people.

My Only Client:

During a year of economic recession and poor business I had one very large client-my only client. All eyes were focused on how we were doing with this very large and complex piece of business.

As the key relationship manager for our company, my key contact at the client site was a very draining and volatile woman with a very bad temper. She was my very important and very draining person with whom I had to have almost daily stressful encounters. The more desperate I was for the business, the more abusive this client seemed to be. Motivating my account team was becoming impossible.

One day, after a very volatile exchange I had to express my inability to cope with this abusive attitude and offered to resign and even cancel the whole deal. In anger she left the office as I began to think of what might be the end of my career.

The next day she called a meeting with my boss during which she apologized for the way she had been dealing with my team and me. With emotional sincerity she complimented me for my integrity and the value of the trust she had in me. My very important, very draining person became one of my best business friends for many years thereafter.

My Negative Boss:

Through my thirty-eight year career I have had many bosses. Some were excellent; others not so good. Let me tell you about "Joe" (not his real name). Joe used to say that he "liked to play the role of the devil's advocate". Anytime I had a good idea he would say, "Let me be the devil's advocate". Then he would proceed to point out all the rational and irrational reasons why things would not work out and why I would surely fail. He was very skilled in uncovering all the negatives and making the brightest day dark. One day when Joe commented "Let me be the devil's advocate," I reached my fill with Joe. In frustration I said, "You know, I never liked the devil and I do not want to work in hell."

Joe was one of my important and draining people. I had no chance of changing his attitude. My only option was to look for another job. I am glad I did.

Here you have three examples of important but draining people. Three different methods of approach you can use: ***avoid, confront and change what you can.***

Baha Habashy, Author

In dealing with the draining people you need to avoid them, reduce your exposure to their draining behavior or remove yourself from their life circumstances. Fortunately, if you focus on your important and teachable people your life will be so full that the draining people will find it hard to have access to your life.

Exercise

In Template C at the end of this chapter:

- Take time to list five important people in your life. Indicate reasons why they are important to you as well as the most important role or roles **THEY** play in your life.
- In a similar manner list five teachable people in your life. Again indicate why they are important to you as well as the most important role or roles **YOU** play in their life.
- If you wish, list five draining people in your life. Again indicate the reason why they are draining to you as well as the role **THEY** play in your life.

Please note: You may find this awkward in the beginning. **Please do not let this hold you back. Remember your goal is progress, not perfection.** Later on this will become second nature to you.

Summary

- ✓ Your life's value is directly related to the impact you have on the people you encounter on the various stages of life.
- ✓ Life provides you with three different circles holding three differing groups of people:
    - o **The circle of accountability** holds your important people who help you define your roles and are critical to the achievement of your goals.
    - o **The circle of influence** holds teachable people who learn from you and grow through your influence on their lives.
    - o **The circle of concerns** holds the draining people who bring extra concerns to your life and are seldom impacted for good by your relationship.
- ✓ As you focus on the important and teachable people you will have little time for the draining people.
- ✓ People may be important, draining, and teachable at the same time. Using Template C, take an inventory of your relationships to enhance your impact and reduce the risks of negative exposure.

Template C - People Inventory

I= Important T = Teachable ↓ & D= Draining People		Indicate role important people play in your life & Role you play in the lives of others↓.	
I T D	**Person or organization**	**Reason for importance**	**Related Roles**
I	*Margie*	*life time commitment, cornerstone in business*	*Partner*
T	*Rebecca*	*She needs advice and friendship, helps me develop as a coach*	*Protégé*

6 – Filtering on High Value Subjects

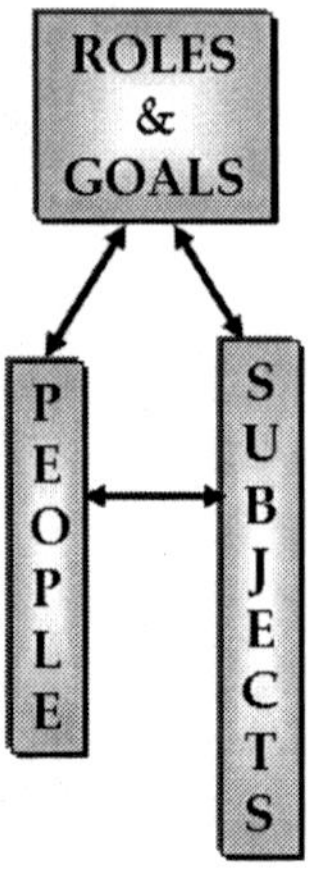

What Are the Subjects That Support Your Roles? *Most of us fall victim to the tyranny of the urgent. In so doing we sacrifice what is often more important. Defining your high value subjects will help you develop an information infrastructure that supports you as you perform your high value roles and achieve your high value goals.*

Subjects relate to the activities we engage in every day. Today it seems that our personal and business cultures are driven by urgency. On a given day most of us are confronted with what appears to be urgent matters that call for immediate attention. They force us to change our priorities, disrupt our plans, and cause more stress than we like. Charles Hummel in his booklet, *Tyranny of the Urgent*, writes "But in the light of time's perspective their deceptive prominence fades; with a sense of loss we recall the important tasks pushed aside. We realize we've become slaves to the tyranny of the urgent." [15] Some of us can cope with the tyranny of the urgent better than others. At the same time medical and scientific research confirm that living under a prolonged state of urgency causes more stress than our bodies can tolerate. The results are seen in compromised health and emotional well-being. The objective of this chapter is to help you take control and prioritize life activities filtering on what is important and not what is merely urgent.

Merrill and Donna Douglass as well as Stephen Covey present some interesting thoughts. We recommend reading their books. Here we suggest grouping our daily encounters into four categories as illustrated in Diagram 8.[16] Plotted against an axis of urgency and of importance you will note the following four:

1. **Not Urgent and Not Important:** These are time wasters and should be avoided and totally eliminated from your life. These are often driven by the unhealthy motivation of giving in to external temptations. An example of this would

be giving in to the strong impulse of having a big hamburger after you finished a healthy dinner, watching a senseless TV program, or spending time reading the "For sale" ads when you have no intention of buying anything.

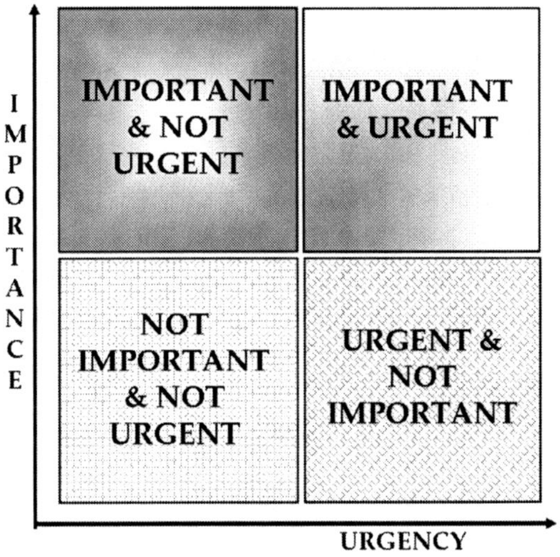

Diagram 8: Important and Urgent

2. **Urgent and Not Important:** These should be avoided wherever you can. Most often-such urgency here is imposed by an external source and is based on someone else's priorities or anxiety. An example of this would be persistent telemarketing phone calls that disrupt your quiet, family dinnertime. E-mail that is always labeled URGENT with no apparent reason for that urgency also qualifies.
3. **Important and urgent:** These deserve your attention. They could be the result of events beyond your control, poor planning or the fast changing world in which we live. An example of this would include a child falling off a bike and needing immediate medical care, your bank account running on overdraft, or a disruption of your supplier's operation that requires an immediate change to your manufacturing process.
4. **Important and Not Urgent:** These are the important activities that are often neglected or overlooked. These often require an act of a strong will and disciplined self-control based on convictions and commitments. Examples of such activities include thinking and planning, coaching and mentoring your staff, engaging in quality conversation with your spouse or child, paying tribute and saying thanks to a

faithful client, acknowledging the goodness of a friend, taking time to energize your mind and spirit...

While the above examples may be simple and clear, often what we confront is not as simple and as clear. As a result, many of us fall victim to the urgent and overlook what is important. "General Eisenhower is quoted as saying, 'The urgent is seldom important, and the important is seldom urgent.' Too often life is controlled by the 'tyranny of the urgent.' We put aside higher and more worthy goals to put out fires." [17]

My current business role requires me to be very responsive on a very short time basis. In a way my current role leaves me highly exposed to interruptions and external, urgent demands. I learned to accept that and adapt to it. For this reason, I had to develop my own screening mechanism to give me some measure of control. At times when I am working on projects, it is important that I do not allow interruptions to distract me. To accomplish this, I find it helpful to turn off the phone or instant messaging or find a remote location where I cannot be easily reached. Another way to overcome the bad habit of constant urgency is to ensure the support of a good team or family members.

If you are like me living in a world where interruptions and urgency is a way of life, my advice is to learn to prioritize. Accept the fact that you cannot do everything. Focus on the two or three things that you are really good at and do not feel guilty about the rest.

Ms. Dale McErlean, Finance Manager

Important and Urgent – Identifying the Differences

Three principles that will help you differentiate between the urgent and the important are:

1. **Important and Draining People:** Earlier, we discussed the value of filtering on people. We suggested that in your life you have important people and draining people. In daily activities you will find that the important people are more likely to feed you important matters or important subjects while

draining people are more likely to present you with urgent matters and subjects.

The important people understand your important roles; they are engaged on your stage and are interested in your success. As a result of that commitment they protect your priorities and filter out the distractions that come from unnecessary urgency. On the other hand, the draining people are not as committed to your goals and less likely to appreciate the price you have to pay as you respond to their urgent demand. The draining people are not as involved on your stage of play; they are driven by the demands of different priorities or stages. So as you focus on your important people, you will most likely reduce your exposure to urgent matters that plague our culture today.

2. **Feelings and Thoughts:** The second principle that will help you differentiate between important and urgent is to examine your feelings and thoughts in response to the matter or subjects presented to you. Urgent matters activate your feelings. They cause you to feel anxious or stressed or perplexed. They compel you to act based on your emotions. They may cause you to feel guilty, nervous, and/or frustrated. Important matters activate your mind and call you to think in a rational ways.

When confronted with an urgent matter, do not respond emotionally. Do not make commitments before thinking of the alternatives and the consequences. We recommend that you practice project-like thinking. Ask yourself:

- What is the worst that could happen if this urgency is neglected?
- Is there any real value in what is being presented?
- What commitments need to be delivered?
- What actions need to take place in response to this demand?
- What sacrifices and costs need to be incurred?
- What is the impact this urgent matter has on my important people?

  Our suggestion is that when you are presented with a matter or subject that results in negative or stressful feelings, bring it under the control of your mind before making any commitment.

3. **Reactive and Proactive:** Urgent matters often call us to react, and place us under the influence of individuals or conditions outside our control. Important matters call us to be proactive and controlled. **Remember, you cannot start anything without stopping something**. There is very little wisdom in giving up something important in favor of something that is merely urgent. Important matters or subjects fit within a plan that is forward thinking and balanced.

When confronted with urgent matters, take control and negotiate for alternative lower cost options. If you focus on the important subjects of life, you will most often be able to negotiate for the lower priority of most urgent matters. Our message is before you react, evaluate the price you have to pay, should you respond to it.

Making a list of your important subjects will help you respond to what is important and avoid what is urgent. This list will also help you filter the amount of information you receive, collect and store. Interestingly, you will find that this will help you build a filing index and an information store that supports your important roles and goals. This, in turn, will help you enhance your relationships with the important and teachable people who are your information exchange partners. As you filter your subjects, your filing system will become an important resource structured to support your roles, helping you to fulfill your goals and add value to your significant relationships.

Some time ago I read a quote about this wise person who when asked about his life priorities said, "My priorities are God, family, then my job. They are in that order because when the job disappears I want to have something left to fall back on". The advice I give to an overloaded person is that the job is important but it is not the most important thing in your life. Make your time at work as productive as you can, (work all the time you are at work) but remember to leave and go home for what is more important and what gives you joy and satisfaction there.

Ms. Karen MacDonald, Regional Director, Quality Improvement and Education

Exercise

Take a look at your present filing system and ask yourself:

1. What information have you collected that supports your most important roles?
2. How will that information help you develop the qualities in the adjectives that describe that role?
3. How does that information help you to DO the actions required by your most important goals?
4. How will the information you collected enhance your relationships with your important and teachable people?
5. What information have you collected that is redundant or adds no value? Can you discard it? Why not?
6. Using Template D, provided at the end of this chapter, begin listing the subjects that you believe are important to your roles and indicate the related role.
7. You can go the extra mile by using Template G **"Filter at a Glance"** which is provided at the end of the chapter. In this template summarize your high value roles, goals and subjects. This handy summary can be laminated and placed in a visible location to guide you as you focus and prioritize your life. Further, this tool can help periodically examine your progress.

Please note: If this is the first time you are doing such an exercise, you may find this awkward in the beginning. **Do not let this hold you back. Remember your goal is progress, not perfection.** Later on this will become second nature to you.

Summary

- ✓ Your life's value is directly related to how you respond to the important and urgent subjects you face every day.
- ✓ As you filter, avoiding the urgent and focusing on the important, note that:
  - o Important people are likely to feed you important subjects while draining people may be the source of most urgent subjects.
  - o Important subjects engage your thinking while urgent subjects activate your negative emotions.
  - o Important subjects cause you to be more proactive while urgent matters cause you to be more reactive.
- ✓ As you focus on your important subjects you will be able to filter not only your activities but also the information you receive.
- ✓ As you focus on the important subjects you can build a filing index of your information system that supports your important roles and enhances your relationship with the important people around you.
- ✓ Developing a "Filter at a Glance" summary will help you focus, prioritize and review your progress.

Template D - Subjects Inventory

Main Subject Sub subject Sub / Sub Subject	Related Roles
Ex: *Leadership*	*Speaker,* *Advisor, Coach*
Coaching	*Advisor*
Tools	*Coaching*

Template G: Filter at a Glance

Role	To (BE) Adjectives	To (DO) Goals Achievements	Important People	Subjects
Coach	*Knowledgeable, Wise, Available, Disciplined, Committed*	*Coach 3 teachable people in work life balance by June 09*	*Rebecca, Sam, Adam*	*Leadership, Management, Tools*

7 – Have a Mission Statement

Do You Need a Mission Statement? *Corporations large and small develop mission statements to help them focus and communicate who they are and what they do best. A mission statement gives you focus in the face of conflicting opportunities and demands. Here are some tips to guide you in developing your mission statement.*

Corporations interact and communicate with a vast number of individuals and other corporate entities. Corporate leaders are confronted with a multitude of demands and often, conflicting opportunities. To help them prioritize their investments, develop their resources and focus their activities they rely on mission statements supported by clear objectives and operating practices. These helpful tools serve to energize and focus corporate efforts on what they do best and what they want to be known for. Further, mission statements help corporate managers prioritize conflicting demands in the face of limited resources.

Investing in a mission statement or what is sometimes referred to as a purpose statement will help you articulate clear, concise answers to the following questions:

1. What are the core values that motivate you?
2. How do you describe the important roles you play in life?
3. What key accomplishments do you want to be known, or remembered for?
4. What individuals or groups of people do you want to impact the most and how?

If you have invested time defining the filtering system described in the previous chapters you are well on your way to developing your mission statement. Let us take a moment and see how the Roles, Goals, People, and Subject filter can help you develop your Mission Statement. We will try to do this by relating the filter to the key questions above.

1. **What are the core values that motivate you?** Stated differently, what inspires your imagination, dreams, and desire to excel? What delivers the greatest moments of fulfillment,

satisfaction, and joy in your life? As you think of these moments try to understand why they seem to be so precious and valuable to you. Picture the stage on which you performed these roles. Try to identify the roles you played during these encounters or situations and describe them clearly. As you do this you most likely will identify the core values that drive you. Be sure to write your impressions.

2. How do you describe the important roles you play in life? If you completed the roles inventory we described earlier, you will likely note that the most important roles you want to play will be a reflection of what gives you greatest fulfillment and the values you hold dearly. Take time and simply list the most valuable roles you want to play in life. For each role list the most important adjectives that describe this role. Adjectives are a reflection of how you wish to be seen and the character attributes for which you want to be famous. It may be helpful to think of the people you admire who fit this role and the key adjectives that describe them. Study and meditate on these adjectives and descriptions. Choose the ones that mean the most to you. Be sure to write your thoughts clearly.

3. What key accomplishments do you want to be known for or remembered for? Earlier we discussed the need to define SMART goals for each of your important roles.. **SMART** goals are **S**pecific, **M**easurable, **A**greed upon by the important people, **R**ealistic and **T**ime dependent. These goals will help you understand the accomplishments you aim to deliver in your life. They highlight the tangible and non-tangible deliverables that you deem important. The subjects and the information you collect and prioritize often impact the goals you want to achieve. Don't forget to write your thoughts down.

4. Who are the individuals or groups of people you want to impact the most in life? The important people are the people who help you define your roles and are critical to the achievement of your goals. Who are these individuals that impact your character and cause you to do your best for them? Who are the people that energize you, either by their character attributes or the compelling needs and opportunities they present to you? Now that you have identified these individuals or groups ask yourself a very important question, **"If asked**

about me, what do I wish these people would say?" If given the opportunity to pay tribute to me, what commentary do I wish they would give? Write down your thoughts.

The answers you wrote to the four points above will give you all the information you need to write your own mission statement. Remember, a personal mission statement is **primarily a statement to you**. It does not need to be perfect but it must be clear, motivating and above all, it must be an honest reflection of what you are or want to be.

Most of us live with corporate employers as well as social and religious organizations without fully embracing the mission statements of such organizations. This is especially true in large multi-national bodies where the mission statement serves senior leaders well but loses its impact as it filters down to regional or departmental organizations and individuals. In such cases it is helpful for the regional or departmental leaders to take time in modifying the corporate mission statement so that it relates most fully to the roles, goals, and functions of the departments and individuals they seek to lead.

"I want to have a mission statement to help me focus and prioritize – a statement that helps me define a meaning for my life. I am working towards developing a mission statement that reflects my beliefs and values – a statement that articulates my priorities as well as the critical roles I have in life."

Mr. Paul Kim, Manager of Finance

We all can fall victims to roles overload. I prioritize my roles by focusing on my mission statement. My mission statement provides me with an umbrella that guides me and helps me focus on my reasons for existence. Based on who I am and what I want to be as well as based on understanding my strengths, beliefs and passions, I developed my mission statement that says:

"I will use all the talents I have been given in the service of others to increase their self-worth, reduce their suffering, and uncover their virtues. I will make a positive difference in each life I encounter."

Ms. Karen MacDonald, Regional Director, Quality, Education

During a time of business and emotional crisis in my life, I started reading an excellent book, Strategy for Living, by Edward R. Dayton and Ted W. Engstrom.[18] *As I grappled with my confused thoughts about who I was and what I was doing, things began to crystallize into clearer values, roles, and goals. Out of that exercise came a Mission Statement that reflected my faith, relationships, and priorities.*

While this mission statement has evolved and changed over the years its core has remained the same. In the following I offer it to you as an ***imperfect example*** *of a structure that you may find helpful. I hasten to say that while it has helped me focus during times of confusion, I have often fallen far short of fulfilling its spirit and objectives. This proves I am not perfect.*

MY MISSION IS:

To know and worship God, so that my life may reflect His character

To joyfully do His will, by caring for:

- His temple (me and my talents)
- Those He places in relationship to me
- My position as His steward, and
- My time, as His life in me.

IN MY ROLE AS:

- **A Husband,** I will do my part in an interdependent relationship that will seek the development of my wife
- **A Father,** I will model a godly character, and do my best in encouraging my children in reaching their maximum development potential
- **A Friend & (Family),** I will cultivate mutually beneficial relationships with those who are important to me
- **A Business Man,** I will work "as unto God", helping overloaded leaders and knowledge workers to have a positive impact on the world around us
- **A Server,** I will seek no earthly reward as I invest my life in those who need the message of God's love

Baha Habashy, Author

Exercise

1. As an example, examine the above mission statements and other mission statements that you may find.
2. Block two to three hours of uninterrupted time when you can think clearly.
3. Find a quiet place that you consider a favorite thinking spot.
4. Bring blank paper, a pencil, eraser or whatever you find helpful to write your thoughts and change them, with ease.
5. On separate sheets write each of the following headings:
   a. The core values that motivate me are:
   b. The following are my most important roles and the best adjectives that describe them:
   c. The key accomplishments that I want to be known or remembered for are:
   d. The individuals or groups that I want to impact the most by my accomplishments are:
   e. The tribute I wish these people would say about me would be:
6. Once you have completed the above statements try to summarize your thoughts into short sentences that tie them together and have the most meaning for you.

Please note: If this is the first time you are doing such an exercise, you may find this awkward in the beginning. **Please do not let this hold you back. Remember your goal is progress, not perfection.** Later on this will become second nature to you.

Summary

- ✓ Corporate leaders rely on mission statements to communicate and prioritize.
- ✓ Personal Mission Statements motivate individuals to prioritize and excel in what they value and in what they want to be known for and remembered.
- ✓ Leveraging your priority based filtering system can develop a mission statement that is tailored to your specific needs and potential.
- ✓ When writing a statement be sure that it communicates clearly and honestly to you personally. It is personal.
- ✓ If you are part of a large organization modify the corporate mission statement by relating it to your own values and distinctions.

PART THREE:

CONTROLLING SOURCES OF OVERLOAD

- Controlling E-mail Overload
- Controlling Telephone Overload
- Controlling Meeting Overload
- Controlling Interruption Overload
- Controlling Paper Overload

Part Three: Controlling Sources of Overload

How Can You Control the Floodgates That Overload Your World? *Martin Luther told us, "I cannot keep a bird from flying over my head. But I can certainly keep it from nesting in my hair or from biting my nose off." Using practical thoughts and tips we will show you how to control the sources of overload.*

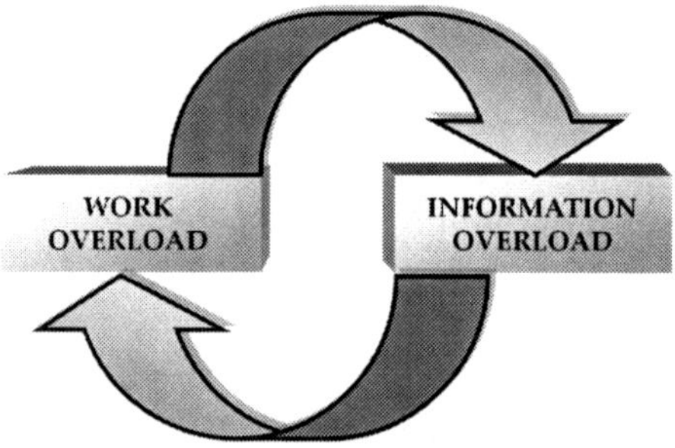

Interdependency, Work, and Information Overload

In a knowledge based economy, as illustrated in this diagram, leaders and knowledge workers face a highly interdependent relationship between work overload and information overload. Here, our objective is to help you identify the sources of information overload and control them. We believe that as you manage the sources of information overload you can control work overload as a natural by-product. As knowledge workers, information enters your world in various ways. The most common are: **e-mail, telephone, paper, and meetings** including one-on-one encounters and **interruptions**. In the coming chapters we will provide some thoughts and tips on how to deal practically and easily with each of these.

Just as with previous sections of this book, please note that we are not presenting a program or a system but a set of "Lego" building blocks. Select what is most appropriate for you and what you can adapt to suit your own needs and style. There will always be exceptions to every rule. Do not let concerns for the exceptions direct and limit your thinking or your personal search for solutions.

Our minds have an amazing capacity to capture images and events and to retain them. Our minds can be likened to a camera that is always on. Everything that comes into our world through our senses is captured and stored indefinitely. The more we focus on an issue, data, or image, the deeper it is ingrained in our minds. Each of these exposures consumes mental energy and occupies storage space in our brain.

As another illustration, our minds are also like a disk drive on a computer. Scientists believe that even before our birth the mind captures sounds and memories of the world around us. This continues without ever deleting anything. Over time our data storage becomes crowded and overloaded. Regretfully, science has not found any delete buttons allowing us to purge our brains of unnecessary clutter.

One of the symptoms of information overload is difficulty in recalling people's names and details. While aging may be a factor, a key reason is our overcrowded minds. Just like accessing data on a heavily loaded disk drive or finding a document in a disorganized filing cabinet, recalling details from the vast quantity of data stored in our minds takes time and mental energy. This explains the reason why small children can recall details faster than older people. This happens primarily because their storage banks are still uncluttered by the huge amount of exposures accumulated with every passing year.

Ancient Answers to the Information Overload Problem

About 1000 BC *– King Solomon, the wisest man who ever lived, said "Be warned: there is no end of opinions ready to be expressed. Studying them can go on forever and become very exhausting!" Ecclesiastes: 12:12*

About 60 - 65 AD *– Saint Paul instructs his student, Timothy, saying, "Avoid the idle babblings and contradictions of what is falsely called knowledge." 1Timothy: 6:20*

So what can you do?

Hundreds of years ago Martin Luther said, "I cannot keep a bird from flying over my head. But I can certainly keep it from nesting in my hair or from biting my nose off."[19] Just as you can prevent flying birds from making a nest in your hair you can prevent information exposure from settling in your mind **by tackling it at the source**. Our strategy for controlling the information overload is to attack the sources of unnecessary information before they cement their exposure taking more space and mental energy.

In the coming sections we will give tips for each of the five information sources we referred to earlier. But before we do this, let us share four common tips that apply to all of them. Later, we will highlight these common tips giving you examples of how they apply in your day-to-day life.

<u>**First Common Tip:**</u> **Define your communication protocol** and communicate it to your important people. What do we mean by a communication protocol? A protocol is an expected code of conduct or behavior that governs our interactions. For example, when you meet someone in the morning you expect him or her to give a greeting such as "Good morning". If you invite someone to a meeting you expect him or her to attend or express regrets. In years past, when you called someone's office you expected a person to answer the phone. That was in the past. Now, the protocol has changed. Today, more likely, you expect to leave a message on a telephone answering machine hoping that your call will be returned. If there is no answering machine you feel disappointed or frustrated because your communication protocol has been violated.

From the preceding examples, you will note that, in the absence of agreed-upon standards or social norms, protocol is largely defined by the expectations of the originator. Such expectations may not be compatible with your circumstances and life priorities. Therefore, it is important to define a personal communication protocol compatible with your high value roles. This protocol should be based on reasonable priorities and expectations. To avoid any misunderstanding this protocol should be clearly communicated to your important people.

<u>**Second Common Tip:**</u> **Seek the support of your important people for your new communication protocol.** If you have ever tried dieting or losing weight you know that this

requires commitment and discipline. You also know that success in such disciplines is made easier when you have the support of the important people in your life. Overcoming overload in an overloaded world is not easy. Overcoming information and work addiction will require changed attitudes and priorities that are made easier if you have the support of your important people.

Your new communication protocols will most likely result in changed behavior. Change is often difficult especially if it requires modified behavior on the part of others. With this in view, it is critical that you negotiate for the support of your important people as you implement your new communication protocol.

Third Common Tip: Batch process because this is more efficient. Years back computer memory and processing power were very expensive. Programmers were very careful not to be wasteful in the use of system resources. As a result, systems were programmed and used in a batch-processing mode. As technology became more abundant and cheap we moved to a high demand, multitasking processing environment. This is often wasteful and less efficient in terms of system resource utilization.

Regretfully, our human mind has a finite capacity. Being stretched and overtaxed we need to move back to a more efficient processing model - batch processing. Try it. You will like it.

The concept of "Batch Processing" is to group similar functions into one common, easy to administer process. This common process helps you concentrate on one type of activity at a time. This, by nature, allows the mind to focus and be more efficient. As you practice batch processing, you become better at estimating the amount of time required to complete such activities. You become better at completing tasks on schedule. This will enhance your confidence and your effectiveness. In the following chapters we will give you examples of how to batch process e-mail, phone calls, paper and even meetings and interruptions.

<u>Fourth Common Tip:</u> Make it a habit; it becomes easier. Those of us who commit to an exercise program know that once it becomes a habit it becomes much easier to keep and maintain. Habits, good or bad, are hard to break. You will also find that others are less likely to challenge you or tempt you to return to your overloaded behavior. People admire and respect disciplined individuals. Good habits communicate consistency and stability that result in an element of security and self-confidence. Good habits will help you feel in control reducing the feeling of anxiety that result from our overloaded world.

In the coming sections we will encourage you to develop habitual routines to batch process your e-mail, voice mail, paper and even meetings. Developing a pattern of behavior is healthy and less stressful for you. As a side benefit, you will become more predictable to your team and to those who interact with you regularly.

Summary

✓ There are many thoughts and tips that can help you control the sources of work and information overload. Always make sure to personalize the suggested solutions in response to your high value roles, goals, and activities as well as the important people in your life.

✓ There are four common tips for handling information sources:

1. Always seek to define your personal communication protocol and communicate it to your important people.
2. Seek the support of your important people for your new protocol.
3. Batch process your information input; it is more efficient and uses less mental and emotional resources.
4. Whenever possible, make your input processing habitual. This will make the application of new disciplines easier.

Please note: This section will be of particular value to those who had a high score in the Statements 8 to 14 of the Overload Gauge in Chapter 1.

8 – Controlling E-Mail Overload

***Thoughts and Tips** are provided to help you improve your effectiveness while reversing the negative impact of e-mail overload.*

E-mail has become one of the most important communication tools in the workplace. E-mail volume has increased by more than 2000% in the last five years. This is expected to double by 2006.[20] E-mail availability, ease of use, and low cost make it the most common communication tool in many organizations. E-mail has often become a replacement for voice communication and even all-important personal face-to-face interaction.

At the same time there is a significant downside to this impressive development. Participants in our "**Overcoming Work and Information Overload**" workshop often refer to e-mail as the greatest cause of information overload. Some managers spend as much as three hours a day dealing with the flood of e-mail. Studies indicate that e-mail could be one of most misused business tools resulting in reduced productivity, increased stress, poor communication, and increased corporate and/or personal liability.

The risks associated with e-mail were highlighted in a recent survey of large corporations which found the following:

- 62% of employers monitor employees' e-mail and Internet use.
- 51% of employers have disciplined or terminated employees for violating ePolicy.
- 10% of companies were ordered by courts to turn over employee e-mail related to workplace lawsuits.
- 8.3% of organizations have battled sexual harassment and/or sexual discrimination claims stemming from employee e-mail and/or Internet use.[21]

In seeking to harness the benefits of this powerful tool, organizations and individual users need to cooperate in the development of a simple, easy to administer policy and appropriate e-mail communication etiquette.

The selected policy and etiquette should be tailored to reflect the corporate culture, business needs, as well as its unique legal requirements. In so doing, we suggest you consider your e-mail policy from three interrelated views illustrated in Diagram 9:

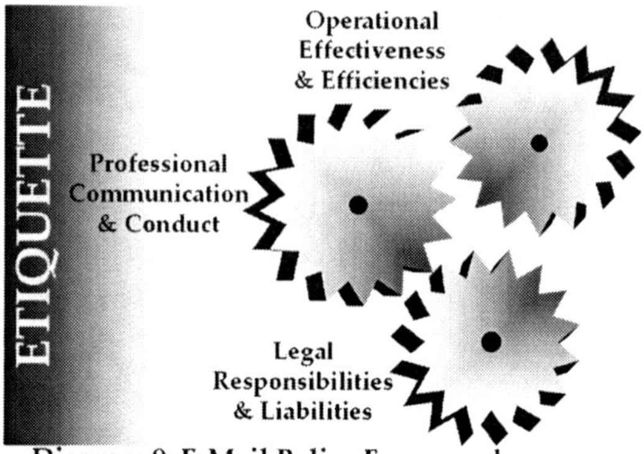

Diagram 9: E-Mail Policy Framework

- **Legal Responsibility and Liability:** E-mail is a communication gateway between individuals and the corporate world. With this in view, it brings issues, rights and responsibilities. Legal minds have not fully articulated what these rights and obligations are. Yet, even today, there are many court cases indicating that e-mail presents employees and employers with significant issues and risks. It is important that you develop a personal and corporate e-mail policy that protects you as an individual as well as the interests of the corporation you represent.
- **Operational Effectiveness and Efficiencies**: Too much of a good thing can be counter productive. Your e-mail policy should serve to limit undisciplined use that results in wasted time, energy, and corporate resources.
- **Professional Communication and Conduct:** Easy access to computers has resulted in careless communication habits. E-mail has become the cause of reduced communication quality that reflects poorly on the image of individuals and the corporation they represent. In the rush associated with the e-mail culture we have neglected most basic etiquette.

<u>TIPS:</u> What can you do? [22, 23, 24, 25, 26]

Whether your organization has an e-policy or not, you are responsible for what you can control. Here are some tips that you can consider and tailor to your own needs:

A. **Develop your own e-mail protocol and communicate it to your important people**. Your e-mail protocol defines how and when you respond to the e-mail you receive. If you do not define your protocol, you will be subject to the assumptions and unrealistic expectations of the sender.

Let us give you an example of why this is important .One morning we had a 10:30 client appointment. When we arrived the secretary looked at us with surprise asking, "Didn't you know that the meeting was cancelled?" "No," we replied. "I sent you an e-mail this morning," she said.

The problem was that our e-mail protocol was different from her expectations. As consultants and speakers, we are out of the office frequently. So our e-mail protocol is to process e-mail once, at the end of the day. We failed to communicate this to our friendly secretary who is used to a protocol where her system notifies her the moment any e-mail arrives in her Inbox. Her expectations were that I was subject to a world similar to hers – a world where the e-mail is an instant communication tool. Regretfully, due to the miscommunication of our protocol that morning we wasted a lot of time.

B. **Seek the support of your new e-mail protocol**. Remember your important people are committed to your success. If you explain that your protocol provides for reasonable responsiveness expectations, they are likely to support you. This will make it easier for you to follow through with your implementation.

Example: The experience described above highlights why it is critical that you communicate your protocol and that you gain the support of your important people for your new e-mail protocol. The following is an example of an e-mail you can use for this purpose.

TO: (LIST) Important and teachable people

SUBJECT: Action Requested – My e-mail handling protocol

It is my desire to improve my effectiveness in handling the flood of e-mail I receive. Towards this goal I have set up my e-mail system to give priority to e-mail directed to me from important people like you. Therefore, e-mail you direct to me personally will be given higher priority and I will do my best to respond to it in ***XX working hours.***

ALL other e-mail and e-mail where you have copied me will be considered for information purposes or given lower priority. I will seek to process such e-mail in ***X working days.***

To reduce my e-mail and electronic filing requirements I will assume that the originator always keeps a copy. ***Therefore, I may not have to keep one.***

Thank you for your support.

C. **Batch process your e-mail at a regular time in the day**. Have set times to review your e-mail. For example, it may be first thing in the morning and again, after lunch.[27] By so doing, your communication partners become accustomed to your processing cycle and are less likely to impose other expectations on you. So, block this processing time in your day as an important meeting with yourself. You may call such appointment a **"processing meeting"**. Be sure to provide adequate time. Start by estimating approximately three minutes for each e-mail message you need to process. So, if you need to process twenty e-mails a day plan at least half an hour in the morning and additional half hour midday.

D. **Apply the "OHIO" - Only Handle It Once -** principle. This is an old, wise piece of advice that is easier said than done. However, if you allow enough e-mail processing time it will be easy to do as you apply the **4 D's** described in the following steps:

1. **Delete It Now.** Most e-mail you receive you never asked for, and you do not need. Your first questions should be, "Why should I even open it?" "Why not **delete it now**?"
2. **Deal With It Now.** If the e-mail at hand can be processed in **3 to 5** minutes **deal with it now**.
3. **Delegate It Now.** If processing such an email will help one of your staff or teachable people grow, **delegate it to him or her now**. For example, if you receive an e-mail with a forty-page attachment or study that may be important, ask one of your teachable people to examine it and provide you with a synopsis and recommendations.
4. **Diarize It Now.** If the e-mail requires more than 5 minutes to process, make a processing appointment with yourself to deal with it later. Be sure to **diarize it now**.

The one thing that has contributed greatly to my effectiveness is becoming committed to what I call quiet reflection periods during the day. Such a time period allows me to process, sort, discard, and organize. Having practiced this for some time now, I realize that giving myself this precious quality time reduces my stress and gives me more control of my priorities. Now when I come into the office in the morning I am not rushed, I have time to greet my staff nicely. This is good for the overall atmosphere in the office as well.

The one advice I give to an overloaded person is give yourself "periods of think time" during the day. Providing such periods of reflection, thinking, and processing is critical to help you process, prioritize and improve your effectiveness in a busy workday.

Mr. Gerry Baranecki, People Manager

E. **Turn off your e-mail notifier -** you know, the thing that rings or calls your attention every time you get an e-mail. This is a wasteful distraction. If you have committed to batch processing your e-mail at regular intervals, you do not need it. If you do not need it, turn it off. We understand there will always be exceptions, especially when you are anxiously waiting for important mail.

F. **Use rules based filtering aggressively.** Most e-mail systems offer rule based filtering tools. Rules are a set of conditions, actions and/or exceptions that process and organize e-mail messages. These rules are applied to incoming e-mail to help reduce e-mail clutter. Further, rules organize incoming e-mail into predefined folders based on predefined processing priorities that are compatible with your most important roles.

G. **If you get too much e-mail, unsubscribe and get off e-mail lists**. It takes time to delete all those messages, even if you don't open them.

H. **Don't print that mail**. Unless you have a need to study and make notes, try to avoid the temptation of printing e-mail. Printing e-mail doubles your filing effort and creates more paper clutter.

I. **Before reading, prioritize;** first prioritize by reading e-mail that is from important people, then important subjects.

J. **If e-mail requires action on somebody else's part before you can deal with it**, move it out of your in-box into a "Waiting" folder. You should make a note in your calendar for appropriate follow-up.

K. **E-mail messages with important attachments can be deleted after you save the attachment** in your own electronic file or hard disk. In this case, give the attachment your own file naming structure based on how you think, so you can find it easily.

L. **Set up a "Reading" folder**. File correspondence from e-mail newsletters or discussion groups in a "Reading" folder for an assigned time to read later. If you find that you do not have time to catch up on your reading, do not feel guilty. Most likely you are getting more reading material than you need and you should be more aggressive in deleting some.

M. **Save administrative messages from mailing lists**. When you subscribe to an e-mail newsletter or e-mail discussion group you usually receive a welcome message with information about your subscription, policies about mailing to the group, answers to frequently asked questions, etc. Copy all this in a document or set up a "Mailing Lists" folder to file such messages so you remember what to do if you wish to unsubscribe from a list at a later time.

N. **Use Auto Archive and Auto Delete to reduce the size of your e-mail file**. This will reduce your filing and maintenance overhead and will help your system run faster or more efficiently.

It was depressing to open my e-mail and find a flood of several pages that are more than I can ever go through. People are wrongly using e-mail as a replacement for face-to-face communication. They often copied me on e-mail without thinking of why they were sending this to me. I made a commitment to take control of my e-mail problem. I use the rules based filtering to sort and prioritize my e-mail and focus on my important people. I also apply the OHIO and the 4 D's principles. Now I go through my important e-mail much faster than ever before, leaving me valuable time to focus on my important roles. More than any other factor, this has helped me become more effective and have more work life balance.

Ms. Kate Agnew, Operations Manager

E-mail etiquette.

The following is a suggested list of e-mail etiquette that could enhance your communication quality. Select the ones best suited for your role and the culture of your organization:

1. Before all else, think of the recipient(s) first. The quality of your e-mail is impacted by what the recipient will think when he or she receives your e-mail much more than what you think when you type your e-mail.
2. Send e-mail to as few recipients as possible. It will enhance your ability to focus the objective of your e-mail and improve your chances of success.
3. Set personal e-mail protocol (etiquette) and responsiveness expectations that are compatible with the most important

roles you play. Communicate your protocol to your important people and ensure that you can support their reasonable responsiveness expectations.

4. Be realistic in your expectations; e-mail is not an **"immediate"** communication tool. It is not intended to replace the phone or the all-important face-to-face contact.
5. Frequent use of the URGENT or the HIGH PRIORITY features of your e-mail is like "crying wolf" too many times. Avoid it.
6. Apply the golden rule, "treat others' e-mail the way you like them to treat your e-mail".
7. Never write e-mail when you are angry or to let off steam. This could be very damaging.
8. When answering e-mail avoid the "E-mail tag game". Anticipate all questions and answer each of them clearly.
9. Avoid the use of the "REPLY TO ALL" feature. Unless requested, give the e-mail sender (originator) the privilege of deciding who should receive your reply.
10. If you are sending a mass mailing, personalize your e-mail using mail merge. If you cannot use mail merge, use blind copy (Bcc). This way you avoid distributing other people's e-mail addresses.
11. Unless necessary for important confirmation purposes, do not request "Delivery" or "Read" confirmation.
12. Avoid forwarding e-mail or attachments without permission. Others may misinterpret e-mail intended for you. Forwarding it carelessly may put you and the originator in potential liability.
13. Define a clear objective for your e-mail. If you can, include your objective in the subject line. *For example*:
    - *Action Request, Expenditure Approval* ***or***
    - *FYI Only, Vacation Plan*
14. Limit each e-mail message to one subject. It is easier to understand and file, if needed.
15. Define a clear goal or goals for your e-mail and introduce this at the beginning of your e-mail. To make your

communication specific start your goal with a **verb**, for example:

> *Dear Joe:*
>
> - *Examine my department YTD budget and approve the expenditure of $3,500 for new furniture*
> - *Advise on how many more $$ I should plan for next fiscal year*

16. Write to express, not to impress. Use simple, easy to understand language to communicate effectively. Bulleted points are easier to read than long paragraphs.
17. Avoid using e-mail to discuss confidential information.
18. If you must send sensitive material add an appropriate disclaimer or a legal liability phrase. As an example:

> ***IMPORTANT NOTE*** *This e-mail may contain confidential information intended solely for the use of the individual or entity to whom it is addressed or to others authorized by them. If you have received this communication in error,* ***please*** *notify us immediately by responding to this e-mail and then delete it from your system. This is your rightful and legal responsibility.*

19. Do not overload the recipient's e-mail by sending unnecessary attachments.
20. Forwarding e-mail containing defamatory, offensive, racist or obscene remarks will put you in a compromised position. Do not do it, even if you think it is funny.
21. Do not engage in the SPAM game. Do not ever forward or reply to SPAM.
22. Careless people may send you "hoax" type messages. Do not forward any hoax or virus warning before validating its claim through a reliable source.
23. Start your e-mail with a proper salutation and end it with a proper signature. It adds structure and clarity.
24. Make sure the tone of your communication including the typeface and font support the e-mail objective. As an example:

- ***BOLD FONTS AND CAPITAL LETTERS are more aggressive.***
- ***Normal*** fonts and simple sentence structures are more friendly and warm.

25. People like the sound of their name; use it in a reasonable manner if you want to be more personal.
26. Use abbreviations and acronyms carefully. Make sure the recipient understands them.
27. Some slang words introduce cultural conflicts and may be offensive. Avoid them.
28. Do not ramble. Write specific points in short sentences.
29. Use proper sentence structure and layout. Keep your language gender neutral. Do not use only masculine pronouns when writing to a mixed audience.
30. Before sending your e-mail read it once or twice. Check it for content, quality, spelling, and proper grammar.
31. Before sending your e-mail consider formatting issues. The recipient's e-mail may have certain limitations that cannot receive the fancy formatting you employed.

Summary

✓ Define an e-mail communication protocol that is compatible with your most important role and communicate it to your most important people.

✓ Seek the support of your important people for your new e-mail protocol.

✓ Batch process your e-mail applying the **OHIO** (**O**nly **H**andle **I**t **O**nce) principle as well as the **4 D's** (**D**elete it Now, **D**eal with it Now, **D**elegate it Now, **D**iarize it Now).

✓ Apply rules based filtering aggressively.

✓ Apply good processing habits to reduce effort and clutter.

✓ Apply good e-mail etiquette and teach it to others.

9 – Controlling Telephone Overload

***Thoughts and Tips** are provided to help you improve your communication and avoid phone tag while reversing the negative impact of phone overload.*

When Alexander Graham Bell invented the telephone in 1876 he launched a communications revolution. In his wildest imagination Mr. Bell could not have imagined the impact his invention would bring. The telephone has become the most common communication tool in the world. Ease of access and good quality have made it a favorite with young and old alike.

Today we are all expected to have at least one phone at home and at work. Even in remote communities the use of mobile phones has become commonplace. In the office world the telephone is a prerequisite for every knowledge worker. Additional features such as call forwarding, conferencing, call waiting, and message waiting add flexibility and complexity of a system that has become mandatory for business communications. Regretfully, few individuals take time to fully learn the effective use of this common tool.

Today business leaders spend 10-50 % of their time in communicating on the telephone. Business managers have an average of three telephone numbers to their names. Along with paging systems each of these is associated with voice mailboxes that need to be checked and maintained on a regular basis. The incessant ring of the telephone demands your attention diverting your interest from other important tasks.

Telephone and voice mail anxiety are common complaints in social circles. Alexander Graham Bell invented a tool to serve modern man. Today the servant tool has become a taskmaster that is driving many to distress and distraction. Let's take back control.

<u>TIPS</u>: What can you do?

Whether your organization has a phone policy or not, you are responsible for what you can control. Here are some tips that you can consider and tailor to your own needs: [28], [29], [30]

A. **Define your phone protocol and communicate it to your callers using your outgoing message.**

- Keep your recorded greeting clear and brief. Clearly include your name, date as well as your voice mail handling protocol. Indicating the conditions that will govern your reply will help set realistic expectations for the caller and will avoid disappointments on his or her part.
- Encourage callers to leave a message that requires a specific response or action. Explain that if they do, you will give their message priority. If a caller explains specifically what is expected, you will be better prepared to respond and may avoid phone tag or back and forth phone calls.
- If you are going to be away for more than a day, tell callers that you will have limited access to your voice mail and you may not be able to respond in a timely manner.
- Be sure to speak at a speed that enables the caller to record needed details.
- For security reasons, avoid telling callers you are **"out of town."**

EXAMPLE: The following is an example of an outgoing voice mail message that you can modify to your role and corporate culture.

*Thank you for calling **(state your full name)** of **(state organization)***

I will give your call priority if you leave me detailed instructions on how I can best serve you.

*I try to return my priority calls within **(X)** working hours. If you need immediate service, please call **(state alternate and state extension)***

Thank you.

B. Batch process your return voice mails efficiently

- Whenever appropriate, screen all calls and return phone calls en masse at a regularly planned time each day. Remember your outgoing voice message has set the caller expectations. Try to keep your commitment.
- If possible, use the auto reply feature on your phone system. This feature leads you directly into the caller's mailbox where you can leave a message and avoid lengthy discussions. This could save you one to three minutes per call.
- As you listen to the incoming message, write a brief note in your notepad along with your expected reply.
- Remember **"OHIO", "Only Handle It Once",** if you can.
- Apply the **4 D**'s - Delete with it now, Deal with it now, Delegate it now, and Diarize your planned or expected action. In this case be sure to let the caller know your expected action date.
- When you receive a batch of voice mail messages, prioritize them. Focus on your important people first. Avoid responding based on urgency only.
- If you must call a known "chatterbox", place your call right before lunch or at the end of the day. This will likely keep the conversation brief.
- Do not offer peoples' phone numbers to strangers.

C. Reduce time spent on telephone calls

- Have a mini agenda for your call. This could save you at least five minutes per call. This agenda should have:
  - ✓ One primary objective and if you must, a secondary objective. Avoid putting too many objectives or conflicting objectives on one phone call for this will dilute your focus. A clear statement of objective should start with an active verb. (For example, confirm the need for a meeting).

- ✓ State clear outcome expectations or what is to be accomplished. Start these with an active verb as well. (For example: 1) Discuss alternative to meeting, and 2) agree on follow-up activities)
- ✓ Leave a clear time expectation for the callback or response.

- If receiving a call, help the caller identify the agenda quickly by asking "What can I do for you?" or "What is the most important point you want me to learn?"
- Keep the conversation focused. Use your agenda to bring the conversation back to the subject under discussion.
- If you have need for constant communications on small matters with the same individuals, use a sheet or a log in which you record thoughts that you need to discuss with such people. Jot down your thoughts as they occur to you. This will form an agenda for your next phone call and reduce the number of calls you make. This will not only save you considerable calling time but will reduce the number of times you need to interrupt the other party. If you train the other party to do the same this will reduce the number of times he or she interrupts you.
- Try standing up when you talk on the phone. This keeps you "on your toes" and will reduce your call time.
- Watch your voice quality and tone. If you are stressed, the caller will detect that in your voice. The person will keep you on the phone longer, demand more detail, and may call you back for reassurance. A warm, crisp tone will make the caller trust your competence and shorten the length of your call. Smiling and lifting your voice at the end of a question will help.
- End the phone call by talking in past tense. Begin by summarizing the call and the follow-up action and promises. Then say, "It was nice to talk with you! Thank you, good-bye!"

- Unplanned phone calls can be classified as interruptions. Handle them firmly and politely. Ask to schedule a time that is convenient to both of you.
- Make the best of your voice mail. Don't let the phone dictate the priorities of your life. Feel free to let your voice mail pick up the call or screen your calls via the digital display.

D. Leave a good voice mail message

- Think about your message before you call. In today's business you are more likely to get a voice mail than the person you are calling. Be prepared by having a clear agenda before you dial a number. This agenda will have:
  - ✓ Appropriate professional greetings using the recipient's name
  - ✓ Identification of yourself and your organization, if needed.
  - ✓ Day and time of call, if needed
  - ✓ The objective of your call starting with a verb
  - ✓ Brief explanation or expected action or request
  - ✓ Summary of point discussed or objective
  - ✓ In closing, state your name and end with your phone number. Remember that the **listener needs time to process the information and write it down.** Be sure to provide a half second pause as you are saying your telephone number. "My number is 212 (pause), 123 (pause), 3456."
- Avoid telephone tag. Give the listener options. Tell him or her when you can best be reached to prevent frustration.
- Where possible, provide the person you are calling with the option of not returning your call. For example, indicate that if you do not hear from them by a certain time you will assume a certain reply.

  (For example, "Jim, if I do not hear from you by 8 AM I assume our meeting is confirmed as planned for 3 PM)

- Do not ask for a return phone call unless you have a very compelling reason for your call to be returned. Always assume that the person you are calling is very busy. Ask yourself, "**Why would he or she want to call me back?**" Be sure you have a good answer that is not only based on your needs or wants.
- Don't leave repeat messages. Your second call is no more likely to be returned than your first. Try sending e-mail instead or speak to someone else in the organization.
- Telephones distort high frequency sounds such as "f" and "s". Pronounce word endings and do not swallow syllables.
- Watch your tone. Without other non-verbal cues such as body language, your tone is all you have to communicate with. Put vitality in your voice. A monotone lacks enthusiasm. Stand up and smile as you leave your message. Standing will increase your energy, and people can hear a smile over the phone. Smiling conveys warmth. Avoid sarcasm and irritation if you want your call returned. Keep an even temper and state your request.
- Modulate your volume. A voice that is too loud is irritating. A soft voice will not always be heard and the listener will miss vital information. Stand or sit up straight and speak directly into the receiver. Do not cradle the phone in your neck or use a speakerphone.
- If you are angry or have something bad to say, do not leave it on a voice mail. Face to face dialogue is more effective.

Summary

- ✓ Define a phone communication protocol that is compatible with your most important roles and communicate it using your outgoing voice message.
- ✓ Seek the support of your important people for your protocol.
- ✓ Batch process your incoming voice mail applying the OHIO (Only Handle It Once) principle as well as the 4 D's - (Delete it now, Deal with it now, Delegate it now, Diarize it now).
- ✓ Reduce the time spent on the phone by having a good reason for the call and a well-planned agenda.
- ✓ Leave good voice mail messages that define expectations and reduce the possibilities of prolonged phone tag and miscommunication.
- ✓ If you want your phone calls to be returned you must have a very compelling reason for your call to be returned.

While talking on the phone I often found myself tempted to do other things at the same time. I thought I was being more productive by say, answering my e-mail or reviewing correspondence. I must admit in doing so I was not giving due attention to the other party on the phone. It shocked me to realize that, whether by the clicks of the keyboard or the number of times I asked them to repeat what they said, this distraction was noticeable to the other parties and understandably, offensive. It became obvious to me that this common behavior is not appropriate. So I made a simple change that removed this temptation. I placed my computer on the desk in front of me and my phone on the table behind me. This simple change has had a very positive impact on the quality of my phone communications. I highly recommend this.

Ms. Andrea Seymour, Vice President and Chief Information Officer

10 – Controlling Meeting Overload

***Thoughts and Tips** are provided to help enhance the effectiveness of your meeting participation, to help you become known as a person who leads good meetings, and to reduce the negative impact of meeting overload.*

Someone has suggested that some meetings are like a funeral, in that it is a group of people wearing uncomfortable clothes who would rather be somewhere else. Yet, there are a couple of differences. All funerals have clearly defined objectives and few things are ever buried in poorly run meetings.

Joking aside, everywhere we go people complain about meetings. They tell us they are overloaded with meetings. In a simple survey among some of our clients **86% agreed** that they **have too many meetings in their organizations.** One American study suggests that more than 11 million meetings are held in the United States every business day.[31]

We must admit that there are good social and economical reasons for these meetings. There are also what we call environmental causes that lead to having many meetings, for example, the level of integration and complexity in our workplace has made the decision making process far too convoluted resulting in more and more meetings. The pace of life in our offices often calls for meetings without carefully examining their need, the cost associated with them or other practical alternatives.

In spite of all the good reasons for our many meetings we must confront the fact that the price for **"meeting overload"** is way too high. Studies report that today's managers spend an average **forty percent** of their time in meetings. In a study of our clients we found that that amount may be as high as **ninety percent** of a regular work day.[32] Some studies suggest that as much as **thirty to sixty percent** of the time we spend in meetings is not productive but we have found that this amount may be as high as **72** percent.[33] This is too costly. This price is often paid in long work hours and compromised personal life.

Before we consider a solution we must first agree on a definition. **What is a meeting?** Some dictionaries define a "meeting" as a **process** of **people** coming together for a common **purpose**. Regretfully, very often we treat meetings as an event, not as a process. Most often it is a gathering of people with poorly defined objectives.

How do you compare?

Based on a survey of our clients, an average manager with a burdened hourly rate of $50 spending 50% of his/her time in meetings with 50% effectiveness in these meetings:

- *Spends 960 hours a year in meetings*
- *Loses $24,000 in lost productivity*
- *Loses $24,000 in lost opportunity costs*
- *This adds up to $48,000 of wasted life.*

How about you? How much of your life are you losing? Find out by using the following exercise:

As leaders, we waste too much time. As director of a very active sales organization, meetings occupied most of my day. Meeting overload was a reality of my life. Many of our internal meetings lacked clear, high value objectives. Often key stakeholders were not present or their roles were ill defined.

I managed to reduce my meetings by about 50% by simply asking for clear meeting objectives and expected outcomes at the outset. I carefully question the need for my participation and see if a phone call or a one on one visit may be more effective. I also apply this strategy for my staff and with my superiors. This approach has reduced the number of internal meetings that involve my staff, so that they are able to spend more time with their clients. They too now have become more careful in clarifying the objectives and outcomes they expect from their client meetings. This has helped my staff derive more value from their client meetings and avoid the vortex of chaos that often accompanies meeting overload.

Ms. Susan Malenica, Regional Director, Business Development

EXERCISE: How effective is your meeting time investment?

- Using Template H, provided in the following page, analyze and calculate the effectiveness of your meting time investment for one week. This is how you do it. Take any five days that are representative of your average business life. For each day:

  a. Add all the hours you spend in meetings including:
    - Travel, preparation, and follow-up time
    - "Impromptu" meetings or interruptions
    - Conference calls and long phone conversations

  b. "Guesstimate". How effective or productive do you feel these meetings were? On a scale of 100 indicate your feelings. Record your answers

  c. Calculate your effective time **(Total time X Effectiveness %)**

  d. Add total Time Spent (1) and Total effective Time (2).

  e. Calculate Lost time and % of Average Effectiveness

  f. Calculate Lost Productivity (A), and record Lost Opportunity and Lost live Value (B).

  g. This will give you Total Loss or lost life value.

  - If this is your lost life value in one week, what does it mean in a whole year? After completing the following Template H multiply the final weekly "Wasted life" value **X** 50 working weeks in a year. Can you afford such a loss?

  - If you like, multiply your loss **X** the number of members in your organization who are facing the same challenges. What would be the impact on your organization if you commit to positive change?

Template H: Meeting Effectiveness Analysis

DAY	Total time spent	I rate this day's meetings overall effectiveness % as Poor→→→→→→→→→→→→→→→→→→←←←←←←←←←←←←←←←←←Excellent										Effective Time
DAY 1		10%	20%	30%	40%	50%	60%	70%	80%	90%	100%	
DAY 2		10%	20%	30%	40%	50%	60%	70%	80%	90%	100%	
DAY 3		10%	20%	30%	40%	50%	60%	70%	80%	90%	100%	
DAY 4		10%	20%	30%	40%	50%	60%	70%	80%	90%	100%	
DAY 5		10%	20%	30%	40%	50%	60%	70%	80%	90%	100%	
TOTAL	(1)											(2)

Lost time = (1) – (2)	% Average effectiveness == (2) / (1) %	
A – Lost Productivity = Lost Time X Burdened Hourly Rate	B – Lost Opportunity Cost = Same As Lost Productivity	Your Total Loss Your Wasted Life = A + B

Solutions

We encourage you to use the **Meetings Effectiveness Framework** illustrated in Diagram 10. This picture of three gears, oil, and oil filter will serve to remind you of this simple framework every time you drive a car. Using this framework, we believe, will enhance the effectiveness of your meeting participation and could help you become known as a person who leads good meetings.

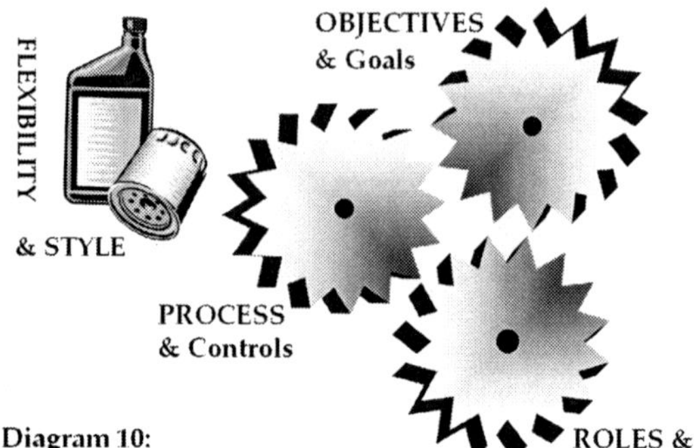

Diagram 10:
Effective Meetings Framework

In the first part of this chapter we will focus on the first two gears of Objectives and Goals as well as Roles and Relationships. While our analysis of these two gears will be of help in your meeting leadership, our primary focus will be on ways to enhance the effectiveness of your meeting participation. In the second part of this chapter we will focus on the remaining framework elements. In these we will deal more closely with your functions and responsibilities as a meeting leader.

<u>First Gear</u>: Objectives and Goals

Often, when invited to a meeting we ask a simple question. **"What is the objective of the meeting?"** A response we often get is one or a combination of the meeting title, a list of the attendees or other explanations of the circumstances for which we need to be there.

Meeting objectives are different from the meeting title. Meeting objectives should be:

- **Clear** - Starting with an active **verb** they reflect expectations of high value that justify the investment of time and energy

Example Verbs List

Agree, Analyze, Announce, Approve, Assign, Clarify, confirm, Decide, Define, Delegate, Determine, Develop, Discuss, Evaluate, Explore, Identify. Learn, Plan, Present, Prioritize, Report, Request, Review, Summarize, Write

- **Few** – A primary objective and if need be, a secondary objective preferably supportive of the first objective
- **Reflected in the meeting goals -** which form the agenda items

Meeting goals should be specific, measurable outcomes that the meeting participants are expected to achieve before the end of the meeting. Meeting goals should be defined in the agenda items. Each agenda item or **goal** should be:

- **Simple:** Starting with an active verb it should define the expected deliverable from this agenda item
- **Allocated a limited number of minutes:** Preferably no more than 30 minutes indicated as (from - to -)
- **Assigned to only one person:** who is capable and accountable for ensuring that the expected goal or deliverable is met

Second Gear: Roles and Interdependent Relationships

Remember what Shakespeare said, "All the world's a stage, and all the men and women merely players". Shakespeare gives us a valuable illustration of how a meeting should run. When you are invited to a meeting you are **"on stage".** Whether you initiate the meeting or not, you are now on stage and you have a responsibility to ensure that the play is done well. By choice or implication you are now part of the team on the stage.

"What do you expect me to BE and DO?" This is a simple question you should ask when invited to a meeting. A good answer will reflect and help you illustrate your role:

- Using **adjectives** try to define what you are expected to **BE.** Adjectives describe the soft skills and talents you bring to the stage.
- Using **verbs** try to define what you are expected to **DO.** Verbs reflect the competencies, experience and/or the authority you bring. Verbs are easily translated into actions you are expected to demonstrate. These can be related to the meeting goals and agenda items as well as the time when your presence is needed.

A clearly defined role will help you:

- Capitalize on your skills and competencies to bring the highest value to the stage where you are needed the most
- Enhance your relationship by complementing others on the stage of a meeting
- Estimate the time and effort you are expected to invest in your role. Remember, **you can never start something without stopping something**. Carefully calculate your time and the sacrifices you have to make. To justify your role and your investment we recommend that you ensure that the **tangible and non-tangible benefits you deliver are more than three times your hourly pay for every hour you spend in such a meeting**.

TIPS: What can you do?

A. Define a personal meeting participation protocol that is compatible with your role and communicate it to your important people.

B. Seek the support of your important people for your protocol.

C. Next time you are invited to a meeting make sure that the meeting objectives are clear and reflect high value worthy of your time. Be sure that you can contribute to the successful outcome of some of the meeting goals (Agenda Items). If you are not sure, make some positive suggestions for change or ask to be excused from the meeting or part of it. Remember, it is your life you are investing or wasting.

D. Be clear in your understanding of the role you are expected to play before, during, and after the meeting.

E. Be careful to ensure that you have the skills, competencies, authority, and/or time needed to deliver your role with excellence.

F. Take careful notes of the commitment you undertake. Be sure to record the expected target date of any commitments. **Template E** that follows provides a practical note taking sheet that you can use for recording your concise thoughts, commitments, delegations, as well as follow-up actions. As a matter of fact, you can use this as a general note taking sheet as one place to capture all your thoughts and things you want to remember.

G. Do not fall casualty to a role misfit. It may be an honor to be asked to attend an important meeting. Before you agree, please remember:

- By seeking to define your **important roles** you will save yourself and others the risk of being a misfit on the stage that could jeopardize your credibility.
- By asking the hard questions of **objectives and goals** you are seeking to use your time with care and wisdom.

Take an inventory of all the committees and meetings you are committed to attend regularly. Prioritize these meetings based on your role and the value you contribute. Remember you need to focus on higher value roles, goals, and activities. Ask to be excused from some committees or meetings so you can use your time for better value.

EXAMPLE: *The following is an example of a meeting protocol communication that you can modify, send or e-mail to your important people:*

TO: (LIST) Important and teachable people
SUBJECT: Action Requested – My meeting participation protocol

Greetings:

My commitment is to improve my effectiveness and focus on meetings where I can add maximum value. With this in view, I ask for your support in helping me practice the following disciplines:

1. *I will attend and make maximum contribution to a meeting where my role is clearly stated on the agenda or I have specific responsibility, or where I can add significant value.*
2. *Please excuse me from meetings, or portions of meetings, where my value contribution is small or where I am not clear on what* ***I am expected to BE or DO****. At such meetings please consider my attendance optional or I may delegate my role to others.*
3. *I will give maximum preparation to my defined roles in a meeting provided the meeting agenda is circulated at least* ***3 working days*** *prior to meeting time.*
4. *I will exercise maximum effort to deliver on all action items assigned to me during a meeting, provided I receive clearly documented minutes within* ***3 working days*** *after the end of any meeting.*

I believe this will help me be more effective and serve you better. If you have any thoughts or questions regarding this, please call me.

Thank you for your support.

Template E - Communication & Note Taking Sheet

Today's Date _Tues___ **Date** _Jun / _20__ **200** 9_

Meeting Title / Objective: *Review new budget process* ____, **Location.** ____*Room B22*_____

Attendees: _*JS*___,__*DW*____,__*KM*___,__*MH*_____,__*SD*___,___*SA*__,________,________,________,_______,

Time		Action Requested		Priority
Type	**Name / Subject / Thoughts**	**Response / Tips**	**From**	**Due Date**	**ABC**
10:30	*DW, Provide new Templates*	*Call DW for sample input*		*6.30*	
	SD, Who will audit?	*DW, expect 5% uplift*			*A*
	MH, What historical data?	*DW, 3 years*			
	First draft due		*SA*	*7.12*	
	Board Review			*8.15*	

↖ Encounter Type: P- phone V- voice mail M- meeting C- correspondence E- e-mail O- other

I worked in the same organization for over twenty-five years. As a result, I became known and invited to far too many meetings. They say that "If you want something done, give it to a busy person" and I became that busy person. In a consensus oriented culture I found myself on twenty-seven different committees, most of them meeting at least once a month. The volume of work that these meetings generated became overwhelming and next to impossible to complete to my satisfaction. The purpose or the effectiveness of all these meetings desperately needed to be evaluated.

One day I was faced with the reality that I lived, ate, and drank work. The price for my work overload became a reality. My immune system became compromised and I developed an environmental allergic reaction to almost everything including my own body. The result was excessive fatigue and I felt as if I was just dragging my body from place to place.

Faced with that reality, I had to reevaluate my roles and what I wanted to do with the rest of my life. My first step was to reduce my meeting participation to where I had well defined roles and where I could deliver maximum value. The second was to seek a new career environment where I was able to set a new framework for new work habits. Now, months later, I am glad I took control.

Ms. Margie Eastwood, Coordinator, Provincial Information Management

<u>Third Gear</u>: Meeting Process and Controls

The objective of the **Meetings Effectiveness Framework** is to help you improve the effectiveness of your meeting participation and your meeting leadership. In the first part of this chapter we discussed the first two gears of this framework. In this part we will focus on the third gear that is the meeting process, the oil and the oil filter.

Again we ask, "**What is a meeting?**" As referenced earlier some dictionaries define a meeting as a <u>**process**</u> of <u>**people**</u> coming together for a common <u>**purpose.**</u> We suggest that a meeting is a **process not an event**.

As a meeting leader you are entrusted with controlling and managing the process. The meeting process is an integral part of making sure that the meeting outcomes are achieved. Diagram 11 illustrates this process.

➢ **Planning:**

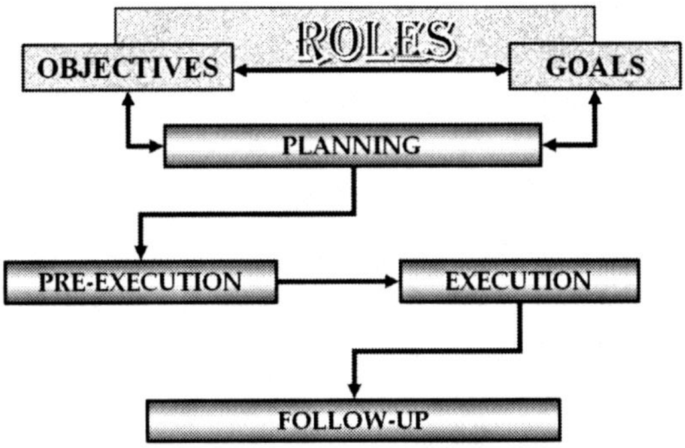

Diagram 11: Effective Meetings Process

As a meeting leader a critical part of the planning process is to establish the meeting objectives. Articulating high value **objectives** will help you communicate and gain the commitment of your meeting participants for their **assigned roles.** As a meeting planner, defining meeting objectives and participants roles could be the most critical, and often compromised, part of the meeting process.

- Meeting objectives are different from the meeting title. Start your statement of objective with an active verb. *(See list for example).* Make sure that your objectives are few and complement each other. Meetings with too many or conflicting objectives:
  - ✓ Take too much time
  - ✓ Include too many people
  - ✓ Are hard to organize and keep on track
  - ✓ Have a high risk of failure

Clearly defined objectives will help you define the meeting **goals or agenda items**. Make sure that your goals are **SMART**. Smart goals are **S**pecific, **M**easurable, and **A**greed upon by your key participants, **R**ealistic, and **T**ime dependent. Once again, we recommend that you start every goal or agenda item with an active verb.

In the planning stage you prepare and issue a **"Draft Agenda".** The draft agenda gives your participants opportunity to provide valuable feedback and suggestions for improvements.

One of the most common pitfalls of planning is poor time management. We recommend that you limit each agenda item to a maximum of 30 minutes. If one item requires more than 30 minutes, try to break it into more than one goal. This will help you keep things on track. Remember, "The mind cannot absorb more than the seat can endure."

- **Pre-Execution:**

In our changing world, the best of plans can be vulnerable to unpleasant surprises. In the pre-execution stage you confirm and try to avoid last minute surprises. This is the time when you confirm the participants' readiness and ensure the availability of all support resources.

At the end of the pre-execution stage you publish your meeting agenda. It is essential that your agenda be sent in a manner that gives your participants one last notice to prepare for their role. With this in view, we recommend that you adopt the **three-day rule.** Your agenda should be issued at least three working days before the meeting date.

- **Execution:**

As a meeting leader you have a complex and demanding role. You are a **host, a conductor, a guide, a facilitator** and much more. Most of all, **you are an investment manager**. Your participants are investing a valuable portion of their lives in your hands. Your focus should be to ensure that all roles are performed with excellence. Be gracious but firm. Control the process not the mind. Encourage wherever possible. When appropriate, summarize the participant's contribution and confirm future undertakings or follow-up actions. Ensure that the minutes taker is left with no ambiguity or misunderstanding.

- **Closing:**

This important stage is often neglected in the rush of seeking a quick exit. As a meeting leader you have the vital responsibility of complimenting the participants on their achievements and contribution. As an investment manager it is your responsibility to articulate the valuable outcome and the returns from the investments made by your participants. As an activity manager it is your responsibility to summarize and confirm any commitments made as well as any expected actions.[34]

- **Follow-up:**

Follow-up takes two forms. **The formal follow-up** comes in the form of minutes. Publishing the minutes of the meeting should not take longer than **3 working days** after the end of the meeting. Minutes published long after the meeting are based on diminished memories and their quality is often questionable. Meeting minutes should list the participants and the roles they played. The minutes should summarize any resolutions, decisions made, requested actions and commitments.

In a separate section of the minutes, discussion notes can be added, where needed. The format and the extent of these notes depend on the nature of the discussion as well as the maturity of the relationships among the meeting participants.

As a meeting leader you are responsible for what we call **the informal follow-up**. As a host and a resource manager you have a responsibility to support and ensure the proper feelings of those who have participated in your meeting. Meetings can be stressful environments where offensive words or actions take place. The informal follow-up is the time when support, encouragement or corrections are made before the next meeting. A phone call or a follow-up visit may be needed to ensure that residual effects are well handled.

Style: The Oil Filter

In leading a meeting which of the three framework gears is the most important? The answer is - it depends:

First, it depends on the meeting style. For example, constituently established meetings are heavy on process. Project management meetings are heavy on goals. Staff meetings and team building meeting are heavy on roles and relationships.

Second, it depends on your leadership style. Your natural temperament will cause you to favor one of the above gears over the others. As you filter through your natural style remember, "You cannot drive a long trip on a single gear." You need to be aware of and engage all three gears.

Flexibility: The Oil

No engine can run without oil and no meeting can run without flexibility. As a meeting leader remember, **"Blessed are the flexible. They never get bent out of shape".** At the same time, if your engine is burning too much oil, it may be time for a tune up. Ask yourself:

- Are my meeting objectives clear and do they communicate high value?
- Do the agenda items represent SMART goals?
- Are the assigned roles clearly communicated and are the participants best qualified for their assigned roles?
- Is the meeting process clear and easy to follow?

TIPS: What can you do?

A. As a meeting leader you are accountable for the outcome and for providing favorable returns for the time and effort invested in your meeting.

B. Take time to plan carefully. Remember to state high value objectives and goals for your meeting.

C. Chose only those participants needed for the important roles in the meeting. Do not select participants based on their titles. Select them to provide the optimum mix of skills, competencies and authority.

D. Your pre-execution phase impacts your agenda more than you think. It is critical for healthy communication and confirmation. Do not overlook it. Send the meeting agenda three working days before the meeting time.

E. During the execution phase you are on a stage. You are observed as a director of a well-rehearsed drama. Control the process but not the mind. Be sure to end the meeting graciously on time.

F. Do not neglect needed follow-up. Meeting minutes should take no longer than three working days after a meeting date. Do not neglect informal follow-up, if needed.

G. Use flexibility wisely. Let your natural leadership style help you shape the needed meeting atmosphere for maximum effectiveness.[35, 36]

I attend a lot of meetings. Meetings can waste a lot of time. I have learned that it is very important to take time before a meeting to think and plan for my roles and expectations. Being organized instills a feeling of confidence and control. I have learned to carry only one binder that is the source of all critical information. In this same binder I have VIP sheets in which I record and sort notes and details that relate to my important people. The same binder also replaces my diary for general note taking purposes.

Controlling overload can be like trying to boil the ocean. It may appear impossible. Choose the areas that are likely to bring you the greatest value or benefit. Focus on these and be committed to make change happen. You will be glad you did.

Ms. Kate Agnew, Operations Manager

Summary

✓ Meetings are critical for our social and business interactions.

✓ Knowledge workers invest a significant percentage of time in meetings.

✓ The **Meeting Effectiveness Framework** can help improve the effectiveness of your meeting participation and help you become known as a person who leads good meetings.

✓ Your effectiveness is highly impacted by:

- Engaging in meetings that have high value objectives and SMART goals
- Playing appropriate roles that complement and support other meeting participants
- The availability of a well orchestrated process appropriate for the meeting objectives and participants, style and an appropriate measure of flexibility

✓ You can become known as a person who leads good meetings if you follow a simple meeting process, filter your leadership through appropriate style, and temper your experience with reasonable flexibility.

11 – Controlling Interruptions

Thoughts and Tips *are provided to help you improve your effectiveness by batch processing interruptions.*

Studies suggest that as much as 30 % of your workday can be wasted due to interruptions.[37] Constant interruptions lead to irritability and frustration. As you try to prioritize your daily activities and focus on important roles, goals and activities, interruptions take control of your life and prevent you from doing what you had planned. Interruptions come from a variety of sources and take a variety of forms:

1. **The phone** has become an accepted source of interruption. Its persistent ring seems to give it the right to override all other priorities. Whether you are focusing on an important task or engaged in an important conversation the ring of the phone demands your attention. So what can you do? Forward your calls to your voice mail and batch process your calls based on your reasonable personal communication protocol that you communicate through your outgoing voice message.
2. **E-mail notifier**: Whether by ring or synthesized voice calling "You Got Mail" this most irritating technology can divert your attention and cause you to waste valuable energy. So what can you do? Turn your e-mail notifier off and batch process your e-mail based on your reasonable communication protocol that is compatible with your roles and has the support of your important people.
3. **Instant Messaging**: If you are part of the emerging world order you may be expected to be **always on.** Through instant messaging products like IBM SameTime, Microsoft Instant Messenger, and others, friends and foes have access to your ears and eyes as long as you allow them. So what can you do? Turn off this feature or restrict access to a very select few only when you are prepared to receive interruptions in response to very important situations. Use appropriate filters to control this most invasive technology.

4. **"Do you have a minute?"** This common request that faces a busy manager can be most irritating when it comes repeatedly from the same draining people. Before your inner soul is able to say "**No**" the visitor has already entered your office and is comfortably seated in your chair. So what can you do? Avoid the draining people. Coach your important and teachable people in batch processing interruptions into well-planned meetings.
5. **Self-induced interruptions**: A self-induced interruption is just as damaging as an interruption that enters your world from outside sources. This is how it plays out. As you are working on something important a thought comes into your mind. You remember something you wish to share with another person. You rush to relieve your mind from the burden of carrying this thought. You pick up the phone, send an e-mail or get up and drop by the unsuspecting other saying, **"I was just thinking…"** This not only destroys your concentration but also inflicts unwanted interruptions on others. What can you do? Learn the art of batch processing interruptions into well-planned meetings.

My advice to the overloaded person is to turn off the electronic alarms in your life - whether it be the sound that notifies you of a new e-mail, or the meeting reminder that buzzes you every ten minutes of a coming meeting, or the persistent ring of a phone when you should not be disturbed. These are distressful distractions that can drive you to despair. Take control over them; turn off what you do not absolutely need.

Ms. Andrea Seymour, Vice President and Chief Information Officer

<u>TIPS</u>: What can you do?

Batch processing interruptions into well-planned meetings:

While being accessible to your team and having an open door should be encouraged, it is important to set reasonable control so you can focus on important tasks. We recommend the habit of using a **"VIP Paper"**. What is that? It is a simple tool that will help you capture important thoughts and record important tips. Further, it will help you organize your thoughts and set the stage for focused one-on-one meetings with your important and teachable people.

VIP always stood for "Very Important People". Here we like to call it a "**V**ery **I**mportant **P**aper for a **V**ery **I**mportant **P**erson". The following Template "F" provides an example of a simple note taking sheet we call it the **VIP Sheet.** This is to help you capture your thoughts for future discussion with your important and teachable people.

This is how it works. Keep a separate VIP sheet for every one of the important people you communicate with regularly. Place these in a divided ring binder. As you are working or even while you are in some meeting when you remember or receive a valuable thought that you wish to share or discuss with one of your important others resist the urge of calling them, e-mailing them or going up to see them. Instead, write that thought down in the "Thought" column of the VIP sheet you labeled with this person's name. Save that thought till the next time you meet.

I lead a large team plus I have other senior leaders that I call my important people. My life is full of activities and demands that are hard to sort and organize. I had to find a tool to ensure that nothing falls through the cracks. Having a VIP binder was the tool I needed.

My VIP binder has a tab for each of my important people. As thoughts or "To Do" items come to mind, I automatically record them in the section relating to the particular person. It also has a section for notes for myself. This provides me with an easy tool for organizing and delegating responsibilities to the appropriate roles among my team. This, by far, has had the greatest impact on my effectiveness.

Mr. Paul Kim, Manager of Finance

Template F: VIP – Thoughts and Tips

Time	Prepared For Discussion With:	*Adam Helpful*	Action Requested		Priority
Date	**Name / Subject / Thoughts**	**Response / Tips**	**From**	**Due Date**	**ABC**
6.20	*Can you help with budget?*	*Excited about role, will prep draft*		*6.27*	
	Review accounting skills	*A+ HS accounting*			
	Discuss holiday plans	*No problem*			
6.22	*Consider CMA course*				
	How are your project skills?				
	Meet with SJ for review			*6.29*	

One of the great ways to enhance your relationship with the important and teachable people in your life is to have regular, pre-planned, one-on-one meetings with them. Depending on the relationship and the need, such appointments should vary in duration and frequency. It is during such a meeting that all the thoughts you recorded can be brought up and discussed. You can then note the response in the "Tips or Response" column. You see what you have indirectly developed is an agenda for your one-on-one encounter. As you collect these sheets they become a progressive record of the items you discussed, an appropriate reminder for follow-up, and a non-offensive tool for ongoing accountability. Most importantly, you have reduced the interruptions you are causing yourself and others.

Now is your chance to be a coach. You can see that if you train the people who interrupt you frequently to follow the same approach you will also save most of the interruptions they cause in your life. This will save you even more time and energy.

You may be presently using regular notebooks for a similar purpose. This is fine. One key advantage of using our approach is that as you keep your sheets in a divided binder you are sorting your thoughts as you go along. You may keep a sheet or section for yourself as well. This would serve as your "one place for all notes". Periodically, say once a month, take out a section, label it, staple it and put it away for your records.

Please note: there will always be times when things cannot wait. Be reasonable. Be flexible. Remember, "Blessed are the flexible; they never get bent out of shape."

The most important tool that has helped me take control of my urgency driven world is a simple binder in which I record all the important thoughts that cross my mind or the important communications and commitments I make. This binder is organized by sections reflecting my important people as well as the important details I need to remember. During the day I take time to examine and process what I have entered in my binder. Some items will lead me to block additional time in my calendar when I can work for longer, uninterrupted periods. This has been most helpful to me.

Ms. Dale McErlean, Finance Manager

This system may not work with highly impulsive or draining people. Let us give you an example that happens far too often. A draining person who often interrupts your day comes to your door asking the same question, **"Do you have a minute?"** Before you are able to say no, he or she starts talking. Here is what you should do.

Shortly after the first few sentences ask, **"What would you like to see happen as result of our visit?"** You see, you are politely asking for a clear, visible outcome. You are helping him or her define an agenda for your meeting. A draining person is not likely to have thought so far. By this statement you are helping the draining person think and take some responsibility for the outcome of the meeting. If no agenda was thought of or if he or she says, "I am not sure" ask him or her to return when they have defined one. If the person has thought of a clear outcome suggest that for best results you would be glad to schedule adequate time in the future. In so doing you are coaching the draining person in the value of proactive thinking and planning. You are respectfully allowing them appropriate time based on your controlled calendar.[38]

As I examine my work life I find that meetings, e-mail, and interruptions are the three critical factors that lead to overload in my business world. The number of meetings and the amount of time spent on items of low importance to the business have to be better managed. Some managers delegate managing their calendar to an assistant. My time is a valuable asset. It is my responsibility to accept or reject a meeting. This should not be easily delegated to others.

I receive a lot of e-mail and I had to learn to prioritize what deserves my time. I learned to filter out what is not from my very important people and reduce the priority of the flood of "cc" that comes into my inbox. These changes, along with reducing the interruptions that distract my focus, have helped me manage my effectiveness and hopefully, give me more time to spend on activities valued by our customers and our business.

Mr. John Ramdeen, Finance Executive, Global Services

I organized the time I spend with my employees. While my team knows that they can come and see me any time, I have structured regular one on one meetings to discuss work and personal issues. This has reduced the number of interruptions I get and has enhanced my relationships with my staff.

I also learned that I need to block one on one time with myself. For me, life can be quite hectic. I need processing time to "think" without the interruptions and distractions of others around me. The most important advice I can give to an overloaded manager is to block regular processing time to think. It may be as little as fifteen minutes a day or during a hectic time; however, it proves invaluable in the long run.

Ms. Joelle Perez, Finance Project Leading Manager

Summary

- ✓ Interruptions can waste as much as 30% of your day, frustrate you, and destroy your effectiveness.
- ✓ Interruptions often result as a response to urgent situations and impulses.
- ✓ Most items that cause interruptions can wait for a future time and a future response.
- ✓ Interruptions come via e-mail, phone, computer generated instant messaging tools, and impromptu meetings.
- ✓ Batch process your important thoughts by using regularly scheduled one-on-one encounters with your important and teachable people.
- ✓ Use the VIP sheet to develop thoughts to guide your one-on-one meetings with your important people. This will also serve as a record of follow-up and accountability.
- ✓ Become a coach helping others to follow your lead and example by not interrupting you.
- ✓ By example and simple questions train the draining people to think before they interrupt.

12 – Controlling Paper Overload

Thoughts and Tips *you will find in the chapter could help you improve your effectiveness by reducing office clutter and paper overload.*

The paperless office is a myth that may never happen. Please consider the following statistics:

- One report estimates that paper consumption has increased by 40% in the last 5 years due to the excessive use and misuse of e-mail.[39]
- In 1992 Kathryn Alesandrini reported that
  - "By the year 2000, U.S. businesses will file 120 billion new sheets of paper a year, enough for 5 million filing cabinets.
  - Nearly half of all file cabinets house duplicate records.
  - The average firm could eliminate one third of their files and transfer another third to inactive storage with no loss of productivity
  - Between 75 and 85 percent of filed papers are never referred to again.
  - Lost files cost at least $60 [U.S.] per file to reconstruct.
  - Each file cabinet you empty saves $600 [U.S.] a year."[40]
  - *In 2003 Christine Cavanagh wrote that "Experts have tabulated that North American office printers spewed out 1.2 trillion sheets of paper in 2001; an increase of 50 percent since 1996."*[41]

Most people feel they need more office and desk space. This is primarily due to having too much paper cluttering their work environment. Paper in your office has a strong visual impact. As your eyes glance at what you have on your desk or on your shelves your attention is diverted from what deserves your focus. Cluttered filing spaces often result in lost documents and/or high maintenance overhead. While you cannot live without paper in your office, you must work very hard at keeping it under control.

In my role and the type of work I do it was easy for me to become an accumulator of paper and documentation. In the taxation world the government has the ability to create and distribute more information and paper than most of us can cope with. The result is that it became difficult for me to easily find what I needed when I needed it. Some change had to happen. I decided to take control of information overload. Today, my office is clutter free. I am able to prioritize, delegate, and handle documents more promptly. I have very few outstanding issues.

It is interesting how this has impacted my staff. Following my example, they in turn have become more organized. In an organization where document retention and timely access is critical to effectiveness I now seldom hear anyone complaining about not being able to find a document.

As we keep the discipline to prioritize and organize our document handling and processing I believe that our effectiveness will be improved by at least 50%.

Mr. Ross Graham, Manager, Taxation

As a general principle, document originators have the responsibility of maintaining copies of all documents they create. With this in view, you need to always examine the reasons for which you create documents or file documents you receive from others. The following are some tips that have helped many of our clients. Tailor them to your own needs. Apply them to simplify your life and they will give you great benefits.

TIPS: What can you do?

Whether your organization has a document handling and retention policy or not, you are responsible for what you can control.

A. **Develop your own paper handling protocol and communicate it to your important people**. This protocol defines in general terms how and when you will respond to the various types of documents you receive. While there will always be exceptions, exceptions should not dictate and drive your rational processes. If you do not communicate your protocol and gain the support of your important people you will always fall victim to the varied expectations others establish for you. These are often based on their agendas and personal priorities.

EXAMPLE: Here is an example of e-mail or a memo you can send out:

TO: (LIST) Important and teachable people

SUBJECT: Action Requested – My paper handling protocol

Greetings:

It is my desire to improve my effectiveness in handling the flood of paper I receive. Towards this goal I ask for your support as I adhere to the following disciplines:

- *I will handle my paper inbox only once a day at* ***(state time of day).***
- *I will give priority to items sent to me personally from important people like you and I will seek to respond to them within* ***(X) working days.*** *ALL other mail and mail where you have copied me will be considered for information purposes and given lower priority.*
- *Further, I will give your document higher priority if you provide a subject line indicating what action you expect from me*
- *To reduce my paper filing requirements I will assume that the originator always keeps a copy.* ***Therefore, I may not have to keep a copy.***

Please ***DO NOT*** *place any incoming mail anywhere except in the INBOX.*

Thank you for your support.

B. **Seek support for your new paper handling protocol**. Remember, there will always be conflicting priorities. Items that others may deem important may only be merely urgent. Your important people will help you withstand the pressure of urgency if they understand and support your paper handling protocol.

C. **Batch process your paper mail at a regular time in the day**. Set regular times to review your INBOX. This could be first thing in the morning or maybe midday. If so, block this time in your calendar as an important appointment with yourself. You may call such an appointment a "processing meeting".

D. **Examine your INBOX by the recycling box**. This encourages you to discard most of your mail before you take it into your office.

E. **Apply the "OHIO"** – Only Handle It Once **principle.** If you allow enough paper processing time, you can apply the **4 D's** described below:

   1. **Delete (Discard) It Now.** If you have not asked for it or it is not clearly labeled to be from one of your important people, your first question should be why should you even open it. Why not delete it now?

   2. **Deal With It Now.** If the item at hand can be processed in 3 to 5 minutes deal with it now.

   3. **Delegate It Now.** If processing such a document will help one of your teachable people grow, delegate it to him or her. So delegate it now. For example, if you receive a forty-page report or study that may be important, ask one of your teachable people to examine it and provide you with a synopsis or recommendations.

   4. **Diarize It Now.** If the document you just received requires more than 5 minutes of your time make a processing appointment with yourself to deal with it. Be sure to diarize it now.

F. **Keep your INBOX out of sight**. This will help you avoid the temptation for distraction every time someone places an item in your INBOX. This is a wasteful distraction that you can avoid.

G. **Keep a DELETE Box**. This is a box where you place items that you wish to discard but fear the possibility of needing it some time soon. Avoid the temptation to open such items. Instead, place it in the DELETE box so you can retrieve it if the need arises. If the need does not arise within a reasonable period, say a month or tow, discard it permanently.

H. **Keep your OUTBOX handy**. If your OUTBOX is within reach you can place items in it easily and access them any time you are leaving the office or passing by the mailroom.

I. **Unsubscribe from magazines and periodicals**. When you get them, clip what you need, place it in your reading file and discard the rest.

Paper overload has been one of my critical problems. I seemed to be overrun with paper, charts, and reports that built and accumulated on my desk. To improve my effectiveness and cope with the increased demands placed on me I had to take control of this part of my business life. My starting point was to design a filing system that reflects my roles and how I operate. It was important to make sure that the headings on the files are easily understood and make sense to me, reflecting the way I think. Now I have a cabinet that contains my key issues or key items. I also have one drawer that deals with my staffing issues and my relationship with them. During the day I move a lot to different meetings. Now I carry a small binder that holds all the current critical data that I need to refer to often.

Having an organized filing system and keeping my desk clear did not only help me feel in control of my world but has also saved me a lot of time. Now I do not waste too much time looking for what I need.

Mr. Gerry Baranecki, People Manager

Summary

- ✓ The paperless office is a myth that may never happen.
- ✓ Most documents in our offices are not needed for normal business life.
- ✓ As a general principle, the originator of any document is responsible for maintaining it. Always ask why you should keep a copy.
- ✓ Develop your personal paper handling protocol, communicate it and gain the support of your important people for it.
- ✓ Batch process your mail. Handle it only once applying the 4D's.
- ✓ Keep your INBOX out of sight and your OUTBOX handy.
- ✓ Use a DELETE Box to help you discard items that you are afraid to destroy.
- ✓ Unsubscribe from magazines and periodicals. When you get them clip what you need, place it in your reading file and discard the rest.

PART FOUR:

DEVELOPING A CLUTTER FREE FILING SYSTEM

- Designing a Clutter Free Filing System
- Building a Clutter Free Filing System
  - **Building Your Workspace and Paper Files**
  - **Building Your E-Mail Space and Files**
  - **Building Your Electronic Space and Files**
- Maintaining a Clutter Free System

Part Four – Developing a Clutter Free Filing System

How Can You Reduce Your Information Clutter? *Studies indicate that knowledge workers spend between 15 to 35 % of their time looking for information.*[42] *Using simple methods practised by professional librarians worldwide we will help you reduce the clutter and the stress caused by information overload.*

What is your answer to the following questions?

- ✓ Do you find it difficult to access data you know is buried somewhere in your e-mail system?
- ✓ When you walk into your office, do you see stacks of binders, magazines, and files that you have not used in the last few days or weeks?
- ✓ When you look at your desk, is most of it covered with paper?
- ✓ When you open your e-mail inbox, is it full of old and new, read and unread messages?
- ✓ Are you getting frequent notices from your system administrator that your e-mail account is running out of space?
- ✓ Is your computer system running slower by the month due to the high volume of stored or unorganized data?

If you answered yes to the above questions, you are not alone. More than ever before, today's knowledge workers are suffering from information indigestion and cluttered filing systems. A Reuters News Service study of 1300 managers found that:

- 38% waste substantial amounts of time looking for information
- 43% could not make important decisions because of information overload[43]

Regretfully, the information glut is not likely to improve. The volume of information thrust upon you is expected to increase with every passing year. The time has come for you to take control and organize your files in a manner that reduces the physical and mental burden that comes from information clutter.

Before discussing a solution we should understand the fears some of us face about filing. In filing we confront three fears:[44]

1. **Fear of making a decision:** Where should I file it? What should I call it? If you don't know what to call a piece of paper, you will call it nothing. If it doesn't have a name, it won't have a home. Such papers end up in unnamed stacks or piled on your desks, in drawers or boxes. To confront this fear you need a clear naming or indexing convention that simplifies this decision-making problem. Spend some time documenting your filing index. Keep this index handy and it will help you overcome the fear of making filing decisions.
2. **Fear of discarding anything:** What happens if I need it someday? About eighty per cent of filed papers are never referred to again.[45] In our fast changing world the shelf life of most information is very short. So any paper you file today will likely become obsolete in a short time. Please remember, if it is important the originator should keep a copy and will be glad to provide you with another copy. So, take a risk. When in doubt, discard it. The rewards are worth it.
3. **Fear of not finding it when it is needed:** How can I trust the filing system? Your filing system needs to be simple and easy to maintain. Such a system will reduce the risks of misfiling and will help you find what you need, when you need it.

File the Way Professional Librarians Do

Your filing system is a resource to support you in fulfilling your roles and achieving your goals. It must be tailored to your personal needs and operating preferences. We suggest a structure that, when modified to your personal needs, can be of great help. It is a structure used by most professional librarians.

Librarians are entrusted with more books, files, and records than any other profession. If you visit a local library you find that librarians have a filing system that is based on what we call **"Frequency of Use Filing System."** This system illustrated in diagram 12 has three simple categories plus some supporting time dependant boxes:

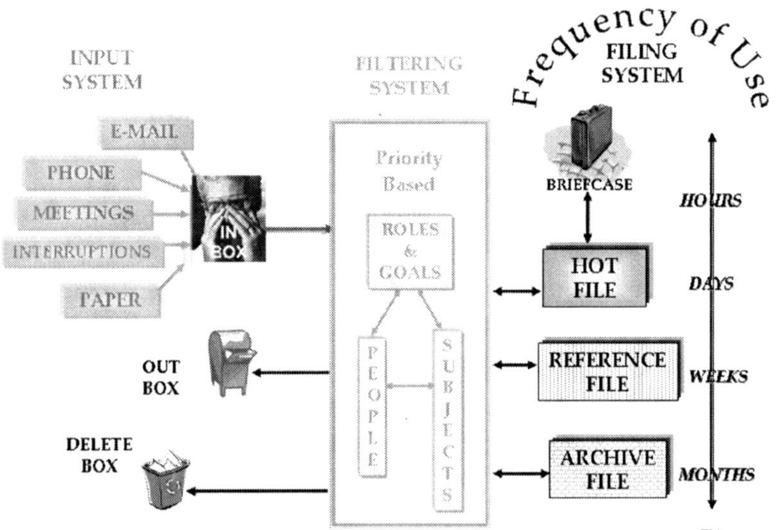

Diagram 12: Frequency Of Use Based Filing System™

1. The first category holds items that are in high demand. These are placed in close proximity to the librarian's desk. We like to call this the **HOT FILE**. This collection is usually small and kept clutter free. Often, only the librarian accesses and maintains these books or files.
2. The second category holds items that are used less frequently. These are placed in the stacks of the main library floor. We would like to call this category the **REFERENCE FILE**. Such a collection is usually much larger than the first. While still well organized, access requires a longer retrieval time.
3. The third category holds items that are seldom used. These are placed in the archives. We would like to call this the **ARCHIVE FILE**. Access to this collection is far less frequent and often requires a longer access time.

You too can file like a professional librarian. Create separate filing categories that are based on frequency of use. Let us call them the **HOT, REFERENCE, and ARCHIVE**. Depending on your need, you can think of them as three different filing cabinets or filing areas. In addition, we are including three other parts of your filing system; they are your **OUTBOX, DELETE BOX** as well as your **BRIEFCASE.**

HOT FILE: This file holds items that you are presently working on, items you need to reference often, or items that require regular updates. This file needs to be crisp, small, and clutter free. Your ability to retrieve a document from such a file needs to be at short notice requiring quick access. As a matter of fact, the benchmark for retrieving a document from this file should be less than 60 seconds in the paper file and 30 seconds in the electronic file.

Let us help you see the picture. Shortly after sending an important report that you had carefully prepared you received a concerned call from a senior executive who had some concerns regarding your report. You have an immediate need to engage your eyes and fingers in this dialogue. You need to have the report in your hand for this important discussion. If you are not able to have a printed copy of this report very quickly you can be assured that your stress level will increase, your effectiveness in the discussion will deteriorate, and the patience of the caller will be challenged. We hope you see the need for this file to be easily accessed so you can retrieve what you need very quickly. An additional benefit is that keeping this file small will reduce the maintenance time and effort it requires.

REFERENCE FILE: This file holds items that you have completed or need less frequently. These may include recently closed projects, annual budgets and corporate policies and bylaws. This file needs to be well-organized and available for access with limited effort. Your ability to retrieve a document from such files may require movement from your desk. Since you access this file less frequently you may choose to have it outside your office, freeing valuable office space for more useful activities.

In some cases it may be advisable to designate a common reference file for a department or a team of knowledge workers. The maintenance responsibility of the reference file, paper or electronic, may be delegated to a special person who takes ownership of it on behalf of the group. This will reduce duplication of records as well as ensure the effective use of this common resource.

Depending on the work you are doing at any given moment you may need to bring items from your reference file into your HOT FILE. An example of this may occur if you are working on the annual budget preparation or a new policy development project.

ARCHIVE FILE: This file holds items that you are far less likely to need. This file holds items that you must keep for legal or historical reference. While such files still need to be organized their access is far less frequent than the HOT or REFERENCE files. Such files should be available in common storage and may even be delegated to an off site location or media.

In the past I considered myself a very organized person. I had all my "work in progress" files sorted in piles on my desk. I thought that having them in sight would keep them properly prioritized. Now I know that this was distractive and counter productive. Now my hot file is placed in the left hand drawer of my desk and on the top of my desk all I see is the one file or project I am currently working on. This has removed the distraction and has allowed me to be much more focused and productive. This has been the one thing I changed that has most improved my effectiveness.

Ms. Cathy Ward, Manager, Human Resources

Depending on the work you are doing at any given moment you may need to bring items from your ARCHIVE FILE into your HOT FILE. An example of this may occur if you should be called for a tax audit, a mortgage renewal or a court case of some kind.

A busy executive suite is a place where paper often flies in all directions. Filing important documents is often neglected in favor of more pressing matters. Due to more than five years of neglect our central executive archive library became a useless resource rather than a helpful asset. Distrust of this neglected system resulted in everyone from the CEO down keeping their own system of duplicated records.

As attempts to rely on external help failed I decided that "If it's to be, it's up to me." As a senior executive assistant I was convinced of the value brought by a well organized central reference and archive library. With management support and the help of other Executive Assistants we now have a system that is efficient and effective for all members of the executive suite. Based on this and my many years of experience I strongly recommend considering the benefits of a centralized reference and archive library for most busy executive offices.

Ms. Marie Darling, Executive Assistant

DELETE FILES: Since a lot of the material you receive you never ask for or are less likely to need, we encourage you to be wisely aggressive in deleting it as it arrives. Be sure to do this before even opening it. Most computer and e-mail systems allow the option to retrieve deleted files within reasonable periods. You can set the parameters for such a set-up using the user or administrator options on most systems. Realizing that you can retrieve an item that you have deleted within a reasonable period will help you be more aggressive in deleting items that do not appear to be of high value at first glance.

You can adopt a similar **DELETE FILE in your paper world.** This is how it works:

- Designate a conveniently located box or drawer as your DELETE BOX.
- When you receive a document that does not fall within your HOT, REFERENCE or ARCHIVE priority, stamp it or mark it with the date received and place it in the DELETE BOX. Do this without opening it.
- If, for any rational reason, you need to recover that deleted paper document you still have the option to easily do so within a reasonable period such as two or three months.

- Periodically, once a month, as an example, take the oldest batch in that file, possibly three or four months old, and get rid of them permanently. Granted, there may be a slim chance that you may need what you have discarded. In this case, the originator should be willing to provide you with another copy. Let me assure you, the benefits of reduced clutter and stress will far outweigh the risks.

BRIEFCASE: The briefcase represents the information you are likely to need in fulfilling your role when you are away from your office or workstation. Your briefcase should hold information you have taken from your HOT FILE. Most of us tend to take more papers to a meeting than we need. Mistakenly, we fear saying, "I do not know" or our motto is "always be prepared for the unexpected". This in fact, can cause you more stress and reduce your effectiveness.

Before a meeting, take time to review the meeting objectives and meeting agenda. Examine your file and take out only the most important documents you need from your paper, electronic or e-mail system. Organize your briefcase in the order of your meetings and related agendas. This will help you to reduce clutter, distraction and frustration. In addition, you will appear to others to be more organized and in control. This is very valuable. Few things are more damaging to your credibility than frantically thumbing through a stack of paper looking for information while all those around stare at you.

I am no longer afraid to file. Before I organized my filing, I used to spend a lot of time debating what I should do with the flood of paper and electronic documents I receive. Now I have one simple filing system that reflects my leadership roles, my project roles and my operational roles. I no longer debate. I have researched my records retention requirements, organized a department db that houses project information and reduced the need to personally file documents. I also have a simple process that allows me to review what I need and discard what I do not need to retain. My files are cleaner and neater. I believe this has improved my effectiveness by at least thirty percent.

Ms. Joelle Perez, Finance Projects, Leading Manager

As you consider your filing methodology, it is important to apply the same principles to your paper files, your e-mail files as well as the electronic files (hard drive or shared drives). Very often we see clients using three different filing systems. Recalling and maintaining three filing systems leads to confusion and increases the mental burden associated with your information management.

The following chapters are structured to lead you in designing, building, and maintaining a clutter free filing system.

Summary

- ✓ Knowledge workers spend too much time looking for information.
- ✓ Information clutter can reduce your effectiveness and hold you back from making important decisions.
- ✓ Many of us avoid filing because we fear making filing decisions, fear discarding an item that may be needed later, and/or fear misplacing items and being unable to find them when needed.
- ✓ Improve effectiveness using a "Frequency Of Use Filing System" including:
  - HOT FILE for items most frequently used
  - REFERENCE file for items needed less often
  - ARCHIVE FILE for items seldom required
- ✓ Be aggressive in deleting paper and electronic documents. Setting a recovery timeline will help you feel more secure in doing so.
- ✓ Reduce the clutter in your briefcase by organizing it in accordance with your meeting objectives and agenda. This will help you feel and appear more in control.
- ✓ Apply the same filing structure to your paper, electronic and e-mail files. You cannot afford to remember three filing systems.

Please note: This section will be of particular value to those who had a high score in the Statements 15 to 20 of the Overload Gauge in Chapter 1.

13 – Designing a Clutter Free Filing System

Thoughts and Steps *are provided to help design an information management system that supports your roles and helps you achieve your goals.*

Developing a frequency of use filing methodology can reduce information clutter and give you access to what you need, when you need it. This methodology is similar to the way that professional librarians maintain vast collections of material and serve diverse demands for information.

Before you jump into the design of your filing system, it is important to look at your whole office environment, contents and layout. Are you comfortable in the present layout or are there more suitable arrangements? What can you do to enhance your concentration, reduce distractions or interruptions? What seating arrangements can you alter to enhance your communication with your visitors? Are you comfortable with your present furniture and equipment or should you change anything?

In this chapter we wish to help you design a filing system that can support you in fulfilling your roles and help you in achieving your goals. In this design process we encourage you to **think and to describe your needs in response to your roles, goals, and the people with whom you interact.**

Most people file alphabetically or chronologically. That is fine. We encourage adding a higher level to that thinking. Diagram 16 that follows illustrates how you do this by designing your filing system priorities based on:

1. The frequency of use of the material you file **(e.g. Hot, Reference, and Archive)**
2. In support of the roles you play **(e.g. Leadership, Operation, Projects)**

In so doing, the subjects you choose for your filing system will become an infrastructure to support your filtering system and the various stages on which you want to play.

Diagram 16: Filing Structure

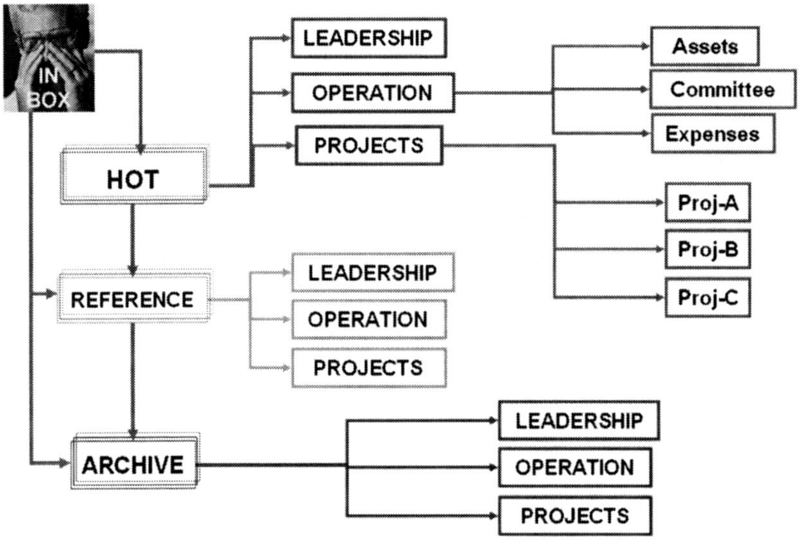

In reality the filing system will become a tool to help you focus and fulfill your highest value roles. This is illustrated by Diagram 17 that follows:

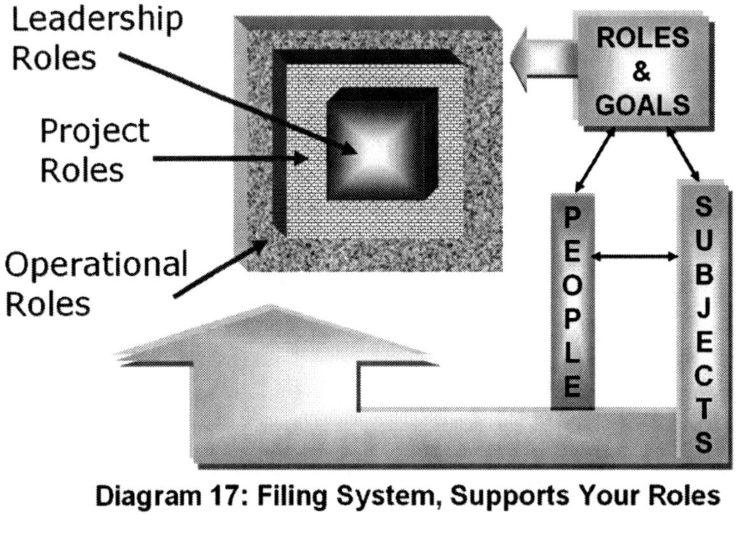

Diagram 17: Filing System, Supports Your Roles

Interruptions had a negative impact on my effectiveness. On the physical side, my office is located in the crossroads of two main corridors and facing the main entry to our work area. Our office building houses over four thousand people. My desk faced the door of my office so I was in full view of all traffic. Greeting socially conscious colleagues was a ritual that repeated itself several times a day. Such interruptions had a negative impact on my effectiveness. Minor adjustments to my seating arrangements and the blinds on my glass wall helped reduce the eye contact with every passerby. This reduced my interruptions and helped me focus on the tasks at hand as well as the guests in my office.

On the mental side, I found it helpful to compartmentalize my activities. This has helped me focus on one type of work at a time, for example, batch processing e-mail and voice mail has helped me a lot. Allowing a transition between my roles at work and home life helps me focus on my responsibilities as a father and husband. This has had a great impact on my life.

Mr. Paul Kim, Manager of Finance

Design Your Work Space Paper Files:

The following diagram 13 illustrates a simple office layout. Further, to help you think of your needs we provided a table where we have listed a set of questions to guide your thoughts. In the margin write yourself a YES or NO answer or comment indicating desired needs or changes.

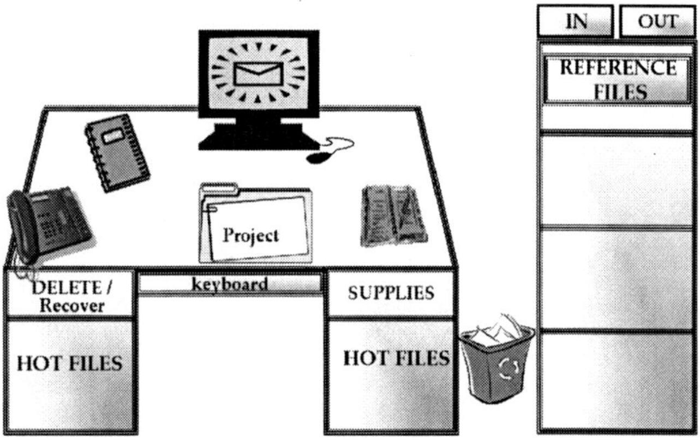

Diagram 13: Example, Clutter Free Office Layout

The following table will help as you start your system design. Consider first **your tangible world such as your desk and paper file**. Being tangible the paper file will help you experience this process in a more concrete way. Later we will relate the same experience to your e-mail and electronic files.

WORKING SPACE:
□ Do you need to change your office layout to enhance your concentration and reduce distractions? □ Can you eliminate any clutter that reduces your effectiveness? □ Do you have adequate desk and filing space? □ Do you have adequate lighting to reduce eyestrain as you read and use your equipment? □ Are you comfortable with your present access to equipment such as phone, computer, garbage cans and supplies? **Note:** Diagram 12 provides a simple layout of clutter free office space.
INBOX
□ Where can you place your inbox to ensure the least distraction and frequent access by others? □ What is the best structure for easy processing of your inbox? □ Do you need the material pre-sorted in multiple folders, for example, Important People, Projects, Literature
HOT FILES
□ Where should you place these files so they can be within very easy and quick reach? □ Do you need a group heading based on your **roles (e.g. Leadership, Projects, and Operation)?** □ Do you need a waiting, pending, or tickler folder? (1 to 31 days and/or 1 to 12 months) □ Do you need a reading folder? □ What subjects and folder headings will you need? **Note:** Examine your present files and begin making **your common index list** of the various subject headings you need.

REFERENCE FILES
☐ Where should you place these files to keep them within reasonable reach?   ☐ Where will you place reference books, magazines and periodicals?   ☐ What groups, subjects, and folders will you need?   ☐ Should your reference material be placed in a departmental or corporate file?   **Note:** It is very likely that you may find some groups and subjects repeated from your HOT FILE. This is fine. These files will hold similar but older material.
ARCHIVE FILES
☐ How can you reduce the clutter created by these files and keep them out of sight?   ☐ Should your archive material be placed in a departmental or corporate archive?   ☐ What groups, subjects, and folders will you need?   **Note:** It is very likely that the same groups and subjects will be repeated from your REFERENCE FILE. This is fine. These files will hold similar but much older material.
OUTBOX
☐ Where can you place your outbox to allow you to quickly place material in it and to provide others with easy access without distracting you?   ☐ What is its best structure? Do you need special persons, department or special function folders?
DELETE BOX
☐ Where will you place your delete files or box?
BRIEFCASE
☐ Is your present briefcase adequate for your role and professional image?   ☐ How can you keep it simple and clutter free so it communicates confidence and control to others?   ☐ How can you maintain consistency with your HOT FILE?

By virtue of my role, I receive and collect a lot of material. My office furniture was hidden under the burden of paper and clutter I collected as a communications director. Organizing my office and reducing the clutter has had a most significant impact on my productivity. Now my daily commitment is to always have nothing that is not filed on any of my desks. It is rewarding to hear visitors' comments about the tidiness of my office. This is not only encouraging but also motivating to enhanced communication and productivity.

In our personal and business lives we each have more than we can handle. Unless you get organized you will always feel forgetful, overwhelmed, and frustrated. My advice to any overloaded person is to develop a simple system to categorize and file what you need, based on your various roles and the priorities you have established. Be committed to maintain your system and that will bring a feeling of control and you will not feel overwhelmed as you otherwise could.

Ms. Shelley Fletcher, Communications Director

The team I manage is involved in a lot of projects. My files were organized alphabetically by project. Recently I was asked, "Donna, are you managing the projects or the people managing the projects?" This led me to examine my role and the impact my filing system has on how I behave. Now, I file by the name of the person managing the project. Now, every time I open my filing drawer I visualize how I should be managing my people, not the project. This has had a positive impact on the type of information I collect as well as how I manage my relationship with my staff.

Ms. Donna Johnston, People Manager

As an executive assistant I have a lot of demands placed on my time. Today there seems to be more paper in our "hoped for" paperless offices than ever before. Frankly, I find paper clutter not only confusing but also quite depressing. Some people, as part of their work plan, have the habit of shuffling bundles of paper from one side of their desks to the other. This is counter productive.

To reduce my paper clutter I have a "Pending" file, a "Probably Discard" file along with a well organized "Reference" file. This has helped me file what I need as soon as I get it and prevent paper from accumulating on my desk.

Ms. Marie Darling, Executive Assistant

Tips on Choosing Subject Headings

One of the key fears we face in filing is the fear of making filing decisions. Where can I file this? What should I call it? This fear can be relieved if you have a simple filing index that you can follow.

For librarians, choosing appropriate subject headings is a very important part of designing the library filing system. Our advice is to keep your filing system so simple that you and anyone else can find appropriate information easily. Keeping your system simple will benefit you greatly as it will require minimum maintenance and overhead.

Here are some tips to help you chose appropriate subject headings. As you read these tips, think first of your paper files. The paper files give you a tangible reference point to help you get started. Later you will find that the same principles apply to your electronic and e-mail files as well:

- The easiest way is to file in alphabetical order within a subject category.
- Use broad categories that may represent sections, drawers or cabinets. (Example: HOT FILES, REFERENCE FILES, ARCHIVE FILES). Then move to smaller categories. (Example: Leadership, Operation, and Projects). Then add sub-subjects. (Example: Project A, Project B, Project C)
- Use broad, generic headings rather than specific, hard to remember words, e.g. "Organizing" rather than "Time Management", use "Financing" rather than "Loans, or Venture Capital".
- Label folders with nouns whenever possible. A single noun is the ideal type of subject heading. Single nouns are simple in form and the easiest to comprehend and remember.
- Rarely use an adjective, adverb, date, or number as the first word (unless it's a proper name or "tag" name). Example, a direct mail firm filed a set of hot mailing lists under the heading "New Lists" but a few weeks later the

word "new" was forgotten. The lists remained lost in the "N" section of the file for over three years.[46] A better way would be to file it under "Lists" followed by a secondary heading such as "New" or "Date", etc.

- A correspondent's name or company affiliation is better used as a subheading.
- Avoid using "Miscellaneous". Using "Miscellaneous" will tempt you to avoid making a proper filing decision and your miscellaneous file will grow out of control.
- Use categories that will be easily understood by others and can give you options to provide subcategories, e.g. use "Banking" then you can add sub categories as "ABC Bank", then "Checking Account".
- Use comprehensive headings to include a substantial quantity of documents.
- When naming folders and subfolders, keep it simple. Attempts to make a folder name overly sophisticated will ensure that you won't remember what you called it.
- Think of each hanging or main folder as the family name. This will help you think of subfolders as children in that family.
- Merge similar materials into relatively few "fat" folders, subdividing only when the folder becomes physically unwieldy, say approximately two to four centimeters thick.
- Cross-reference, where necessary, by adding a "SEE ALSO" note in a visible place.
- Create a subject index or a list of your filing system and keep it handy. It will simplify your decision making process, minimize duplicate files and coordinate the use of shared files. This will also enable others to retrieve files in your absence.

Take time and type the **subject or index list** of your new filing system. You will need this when we move to the next step - building your filing system.

Designing Your E-Mail and Electronic Files

Your electronic files include your e-mail, your hard drive or shared drives, as well as your favorite WEB folders. By now, we hope you have a clear picture of the structure and key subject headings in your filing system. Take time to review this index of your new paper filing system. This will help you as you move to design your electronic files.

E-mail: Your e-mail should follow the same structure as your paper files with some minor differences. For example:

- ☐ INBOX: Your e-mail system may enable you to develop **rules** to sort incoming mail into folders based on your roles and the important people with whom you interact. This can help you process your e-mail as it comes in, based on the priorities of your roles and goals. As you follow the **OHIO (Only Handle It Once)** principle, you move an e-mail message from these folders to your HOT FILE and then to the Reference folders as soon as you are finished with it. (For more on this, refer to chapter 8.)
- ☐ HOT FILE: As you follow the **OHIO (Only Handle It Once)** principle, your HOT FILE should be relatively small. The majority of material should be filed as a reference. You should still have a "Reading" folder to hold e-mails that you have scheduled for reading as well as low priority e-mail. You may also want to have the "Waiting" or "Pending" folder for items that are pending for input from a third party.
- ☐ REFERENCE FILE: Your e-mail REFERENCE file could be the main folder that you have to maintain. Be sure its structure supports your roles, goals and/or important relationships.
- ☐ ARCHIVE FILE: Your e-mail system may enable you to set automatic archiving rules. If established properly, this may reduce your need for setting up an ARCHIVE folder. If your e-mail system does not offer such an archiving tool, set your own folder and periodically move older items from your REFERENCE FILES to the archive folders.

Be sure to update your common subject or index list. Mark the subjects you need to include in the REFERENCE and ARCHIVE Folders. This will be helpful in the coming chapter as we attempt to build your filing system.

Please note that what we described above is highly dependent on the e-mail system you use and the software version you have installed on your computer. So, consult your application vendor for the best way to implement rules based e-mail management in your application.

Today, there are many new forms of business communication that did not exist in the past, for example, e-mail. This communication tool, while helpful because you can quickly and easily send messages to a number of people at once, has also established an expectation that we provide an equally rapid response. The sheer volume of e-mails to process can make you feel as if you are an air traffic controller! To me, it is important to have in my inbox only the items that I need to action. The rest, after scanning, are immediately moved to an appropriate file in my reference filing folders. Less clutter = less distraction.

Ms. Cathy Ward, Manager, Human Resources

As communication director in a geographically diverse organization, e-mail is a very important resource for my roles. E-mail has become the primary method of communication in most organizations like ours. Allowing e-mail to build up in your inbox makes it an unmanageable communication gateway. To harness the power of this tool, I have a simple filing system. Everything I get is filed either by an "action required" file or as a reference item into my reference file. Now I seldom have more than five items in my inbox. E-mail is not a problem for me anymore.

Ms. Shelley Fletcher, Communications Director

Electronic File (Hard Drive): Your electronic file should follow the same structure as your paper file with some differences. For example:

□ HOT FILE: If you think of the folder "MY DOCUMENT" as your main entry point in your document filing system then you can establish a HOT FILE below that. Using Microsoft Windows Explorer, you can build a filing system that mimics the same structure in your paper file. If you wish, call this folder "1-HOT". By so doing, your computer will establish the "HOT" File alphabetically before "REFERENCE" and "ARCHIVE".

□ REFERENCE FILE: Establish another folder calling it "2-REFERENCE" using the same approach. This is to be populated with sub folders as needed and or as listed in the file index that you typed. Note that by calling it "2-REFERENCE" Windows Explorer will place this folder alphabetically ahead of the ARCHIVE folder.

□ ARCHIVE FILE: Similarly create a new folder calling it "3-ARCHIVE" to be populated with sub folders as needed and as listed in the file index that you typed.

□ DELETE FILE: Windows will normally place deleted records and documents in a **recycle bin**. While in the recycle bin, items can be restored to their original location. Items in the recycle bin are erased based on user or system defined rules and frequency. Examine these rules and parameters to make sure they support your expectations.

□ OUTBOX: You can consider the "Sent Folder" in your e-mail system as the outbox of your hard disk data. Remember, as a general rule, for legal and business reasons the originators of a document is responsible for keeping a copy of all items they create. Be sure that you can archive your outgoing documents and retain them long enough in accordance with your business needs.

□ BRIEFCASE: Some may consider an electronic organizer or a small notebook computer as helps to take material while traveling. If so, most operating systems provide ways to synchronize such files for compatibility and ease of use. Sometimes these features are oversold. Be sure to understand how these systems interplay and support file sharing and updates; otherwise, you are likely to be disappointed.

Please Note: Mac users as well as users of other operating systems may note that their computers follow similar concepts of file management but use different names and labels.

Web Folders: The World Wide Web (WWW) has a wealth of electronic files that you can use. Most often you can consider this a REFERENCE file. If you keep an extensive list of "Favorites" in your web browser we recommend that you develop a structure similar to the one you established in the REFERENCE file.

Summary:

- ✓ Ensure that your workspace is organized to reduce distractions and interruptions.
- ✓ Reduce clutter by designing your filing system based on a frequency of use filing methodology. This includes HOT, REFERENCE, ARCHIVE, DELETE, BRIEFCASE, INBOX, and OUTBOX.
- ✓ Design your sub categories to support your roles. These may include Leadership, Operation, and Projects.
- ✓ Keep your structure logical and easy to use; this will further reduce the maintenance overhead required.
- ✓ Follow the same structure for all your paper files, e-mail files, electronic files, and web favorites.

14 – Building a Clutter Free Filing System

Thoughts and Steps *are provided to help build a filing system that supports your roles and helps you achieve your goals.*

The frequency of use filing methodology can reduce information clutter and give you access to what you need when you need it. As you think of what you need and as you develop a filing structure that supports your roles and, be sure to type a clear subject index and keep it handy for you and others to refer to. In this chapter we will show you an example of a step-by-step **action plan** to help you build your filing system.

Building Your Work Space and Paper Files:

Again- first, think of or consider your **desk and paper files**. Being tangible, the paper file will help you experience the file building process in a concrete way. Later, we will relate the same experience to your e-mail and electronic files.

A common question we are often asked is, "What kinds of files should I have?" The key to rapid document retrieval is proper labeling of folders and files. If you are not used to doing a great deal of filing you may find the following tips helpful.

- Set up files logically so anyone can find them. If anyone else can find them easily, you surely will.
- Use boxed, hanging files. This allows you to place smaller sub-files inside each hanging folder. Use only one standard size of folders; do not mix them.
- Place labeled tabs in the front of the file. This gives quick fingertip access to the file as you add new material.
- Label files and drawers with big, bold, and easy to read lettering.
- Avoid the use of elaborate filing color schemes. It makes your filing system complex, and may be more confusing and a deterrent to quick filing.

- When holding paper together use the stapler instead of paper clips. Paper clips can catch other unrelated papers.
- As you add new files, update your subject list or index for ongoing reference

In the following table we provided a task list to help you. plan adequate time for what could be a very enjoyable experience. We recommend two to four hours for each session, depending on the condition of your system. Read the following task list and indicate your target completion date and any appropriate notes.

Tasks	**Planned Activity Date / Notes**
1. Examine your supplies and make sure you have all the essential supplies you need for your new filing system. **See Supplies Checklist, Template G-that follows.**	
2. Block an appropriate amount of time for this valuable effort. We recommend approximately two to four hours each time you work on your filing. You may need more than one session to organize your office.	
3. Place a sign, "**PLEASE DO NOT DISTURB. I AM ON A MISSION.**" Do not accept any interruptions.	
4. Place three boxes or garbage bags beside the exit door or nearby. Mark them respectively as **DONATE, GARBAGE,** and **RECYCLE.**	
5. Establish your best office layout plan for improved effectiveness. Make a sketch of this layout and make sure you have all the furniture and equipment you need. Rearrange your space, if necessary.	

6. MARK where you will place essential supplies, inbox, HOT FILES, REFERENCE FILES, ARCHIVE FILES, outbox, delete box, garbage can, chairs, etc.	
7. Remove the clutter. Totally clear the top of all your office furniture including your desk, filing cabinets, and chairs. Place unwanted clutter out of sight in one of the containers you marked in step 4.	
8. EMPTY the contents of the space you allocated to be used for your HOT FILE. Place it on top of your desk. Add all other paper you had on or around your desk. 9. Label that space as **HOT FILES**.	
10. Examine your subject list, label appropriate hanging folders and sub-folders and place them in the space you marked HOT FILES.	
11. Populate your HOT FILES by sorting all you have on top of your desk. Mark additional folders and files as you need to and adjust your subject list. 12. As you go along designate two piles for **REFERENCE** and **ARCHIVE** material. Do not file these yet. Just pile them. 13. As you go along, delete, donate, and/or recycle any material that does not fit your new plan. (BE BRAVE.) 14. Continue until you have finished filing all your HOT files.	
15. EMPTY all the contents of the space you allocated for the REFERENCE FILES. 16. Label that space as **REFERENCE FILES.**	
17. Examine your subject list and ensure that you have correct hanging folders and sub-folders for your REFERENCE FILES and place them where you marked REFERENCE FILES.	

18. Populate your REFERENCE FILES by sorting the pile you designated as REFERENCE. Make additional files as you need to and adjust your subject list as you go along. 19. As you work on your files designate any Archive material putting it in the pile you called ARCHIVE. Do not file this yet. Just pile them. 20. As you go along delete, donate and/or recycle material that does not fit your new plan. (BE BRAVE.) 21. Continue until you have finished filing all your REFERENCE files.	
22. EMPTY all the contents of the space you allocated for the ARCHIVE FILES. 23. Label that space as **ARCHIVE FILES.**	
24. Examine your subject list and ensure you have correct hanging folders as well as sub-folders for all your ARCHIVE FILES and place them in the place you marked ARCHIVE FILES.	
25. Populate your ARCHIVE FILES by sorting the pile you marked Archive. Make additional files as you need to and adjust your subject list as you go. 26. As you go along delete, donate and/or recycle any material that does not fit your new plan. (BE BRAVE.)	
27. Examine your supplies drawer, donate, and discard what you do not need and organize for effective use. 28. Place essential supplies, inbox, outbox, delete files, garbage can, chairs, etc. where you have planned.	
29. Do not take time to process your inbox now. You can do this in your normal processing cycle, provided you plan extra time for it.	

30. Give your new office a proud look and **congratulate yourself on a fine job.**	
31. Invite your friends and teachable people to see your office. **This will encourage you to keep it tidy and you will help others in the process.**	

Template G – Supplies List

Essential Supplies List	Qty		Qty
□ Binder 3 Ring		□ Light, Desk	
□ Binders 3 Ring - dividers		□ Notepad	
□ Box - business card holder		□ Paper for computer printer	
□ Box – IN tray		□ Paperclips and holder	
□ Box – OUT tray		□ Pen, blue or black	
□ Boxes or garbage bags		□ Pens, Marking	
□ Calculator		□ Phone	
□ Clock, Desk		□ Planner or Diary	
□ Computer system		□ Power cord / Surge protect	
□ Computer		□ Puncher, paper (3 hole)	
□ Computer, Office Software		□ Rubber bands	
□ Computer, printer / cartridges		□ Ruler	
□ Cutting blade		□ Scissors	
□ Date stamp and ink pad		□ Scotch tape and dispenser	
□ Envelopes - 9X12		□ Staple remover	
□ Envelopes for mailing #10		□ Stapler	
□ Fax Machine		□ Staples for stapler	
□ Folders Hanging		□ Wastebasket/ Recycle Box	
□ Folders Hanging - plastic tabs		□	
□ Folders labels (1"X2.63)		□	
□ Folders, Manila		□	
□ Highlighters		□	

Building Your E-Mail and Electronic Files

Now that you are becoming familiar with the process, in the following table try to follow the same structure as you build your e-mail files and your electronic or hard drive files.

Building Your E-mail Space and E-Mail Files

Put aside the time needed for this wonderful, freeing experience. We recommend two to four hours depending on the condition of your system.

Tasks	Planned Activity Date / Notes
1. Remove the clutter by: a. Removing unused folders in your e-mail system b. Unsubscribing from unnecessary news letters c. Examining your toolbars and customizing them for maximum efficiency d. Examine your contact list to make sure that it holds a list of your important people.	
2. Examine your filing index or subjects list. Identify the ones you need for your e-mail file. Remember you e-mail filing should follow the same structure as your paper file **but it does not need to be identical.**	
3. Assuming that **"INBOX"** is your main directory, create sub folders that support rules that you will create or filters that sort, and prioritizes your incoming e-mail as it arrives. For example, you may set up folders called: a. Important people to Me **(-IP to ME)** b. Important People Copy to Me **(-IP copy to ME)** **c. -Reading** **d. -Waiting or Pending** **Note:** By placing a (-) ahead of the folder name you instruct your system to place it first in the filing tree.	

4. Create rules and filters that you believe will help you sort and prioritize your incoming e-mail. For example: a. Set up a rule to place all the e-mail you receive from your important people in the folder "-IP to Me". b. Set up a rule to place all incoming e-mail copied to you from your important people in the folder "-IP copy to ME".	
5. Here we will assume that the working file is made up of the folders you assigned based on the e-mail rules you established above. 6. Now, refer to your subject index and create a new sub folder called "2-REFERENCE" as well as any sub folders you will need.	
7. Create a new sub folder called "3-ARCHIVE" as well as any sub folders you will need. This will act as a temporary holding place until you are sure that your Auto-archive system works properly.	
8. Populate your REFERENCE and ARCHIVE folders by dragging related mail to the appropriate locations. If need be, make additional folders and adjust your subject list.	
9. As you go along DELETE material that you no longer need. (**BE BRAVE.**)	
10. Give your new electronic e-mail filing system one good look and **congratulate yourself on a job well done. Share your pride with supportive friends and teachable people.**	

Building Your Electronic Space and Files

Here, using the following table, we will deal with your computer desktop and hard drive. Put aside the time needed for this freeing experience. We recommend one to two hours depending on the condition of your system.

<table>
<tr><th>Tasks</th><th>Planned Activity Date / Notes</th></tr>
<tr><td>1. Remove the clutter:
a. Delete any unused icons from your computer screen desktop.
b. Uninstall any programs that you do not use and remove them from your hard drive.
c. Perform a hard drive cleanup
d. Perform a disk de-fragmentation operation. (This operation may take some time)
e. Perform a backup of all your critical files</td><td></td></tr>
<tr><td>2. Open Windows Explorer. (Users of other operating systems will find similarities but please also consider the differences.)</td><td></td></tr>
<tr><td>3. Assuming that "MY DOCUMENTS" is your main directory, build 3 new folders:<table><tr><td>1 - HOT</td><td>2- REFERENCE</td><td>3 - ARCHIVE</td></tr></table></td><td></td></tr>
<tr><td>4. Examine your index or subject list. In the HOT directory build sub-directories and folders that support your subject list. Remember your electronic filing should follow the same structure as your paper file but it does not need to be identical.</td><td></td></tr>
<tr><td>5. Populate your HOT folders by dragging related files to the appropriate locations. If need be, create additional folders and adjust your subject list. As you go along move REFERENCE FILES and Archive material to the REFERENCE and ARCHIVE directories.
6. As you go along DELETE material that you no longer need. (BE BRAVE.)</td><td></td></tr>
<tr><td>7. Examine your subject list. In the REFERENCE directory build sub-directories and folders that support your subject list.</td><td></td></tr>
</table>

8. Populate your REFERENCE folders by dragging related files that you placed earlier in that main heading to the appropriate folders and locations. If need be, make additional folders and adjust your subject list. 9. As you go along DELETE material that you no longer need. **(BE BRAVE.)**	
10. Examine your index or subject list. In the ARCHIVE directory build sub-directories and folders that support your subject list.	
11. Populate your ARCHIVE folders by dragging related files you placed earlier in that category to the appropriate locations. If need be, make additional folders and adjust your subject list. 12. As you go along DELETE material that you no longer need. **(BE BRAVE.)**	
13. Delete any unused or redundant folders.	
4. Re-examine your files index for consistency in naming conventions. Make the necessary changes.	
14. Give your new electronic filing system one good look and **congratulate yourself on a job well done. Share your pride with your supportive and teachable people.**	

If you follow this suggestion, you will note that the folders where you file your documents, "**My Documents**", for example, may look something like Diagram 18 at the end of this chapter.

Summary

- ✓ Using the step-by-step instructions provided, start building your tangible workspace and paper file to gain a concrete prospective of the process and needed actions.
- ✓ Place your office furniture and equipment in a manner that enhances access and effectiveness. Build your HOT, REFERENCE, and ARCHIVE paper files.
- ✓ Remove all clutter from your e-mail system, build rules to sort your incoming mail into HOT folders, populate your REFERENCE folders and set up your AUTO ARCHIVE system, if available.
- ✓ Remove any unused icons and programs and clean your hard drive. Using MY DOCUMENTS as your main folder, establish your HOT, REFERENCE and ARCHIVE folders. Using your subject heading list, build appropriate sub folders. Drag and drop documents and files to populate the folders you have already established.
- ✓ At all times delete and discard what you do not need. (BE BRAVE.)
- ✓ Examine your new filing system and share your success with others.

Diagram18: Electronic File

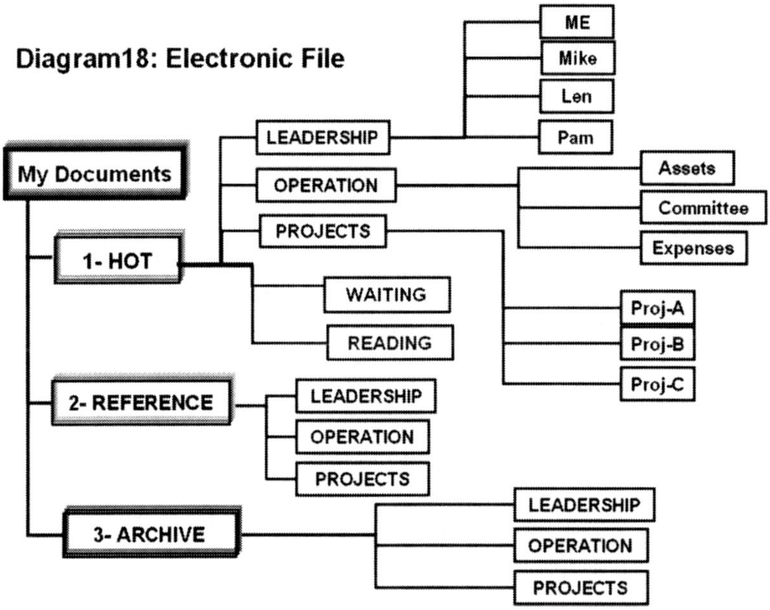

15 – Maintaining a Clutter Free System

Thoughts and Steps *are given to help maintain your filing system so that you can find what you need when you need it.*

Did you know that The Second Law of Thermodynamics (Law of Energy Decay) indicates that that "*every system left to its own devices always tends to move from order to disorder, its energy tending to be transformed into lower levels of availability, finally reaching the state of complete randomness and unavailability for further work*"?[47]

Stated differently, the best system will rapidly deteriorate if not properly maintained. If you do not pay attention to the ongoing maintenance of your system it will disintegrate into practical confusion becoming a liability rather than an asset. Having invested time and energy to bring your system to a good state, you need to maintain it so it provides you with ongoing benefits.

Maintaining your Filtering System:

You live in a changing world. Priorities, people, and your needs change on a regular basis. Periodically, perhaps once every six to twelve months or as major changes occur, take time to examine your filtering system and document appropriate changes. Sit down in a quiet place by yourself. Bring your existing filter including a description of your roles, goals, people, and subjects as well as your Mission Statement. You may also find it helpful to refer to your Information Overload Gauge, Chapter 1, as well as your information Anxiety Symptoms list. Try to identify areas of progress and areas of needed changes. Take time to think and to write your thoughts. Here are some questions that may guide you in this exercise:

- As you examine the filtering section of your overload gauge, how do you feel today? Can you identify areas of improvement or other areas that need some change? Document your thoughts.

- What changes have happened in your personal and professional lives that require a redefinition of your roles? What should be your response to these changes? Be sure to consider your personal health, spiritual, emotional, and mental development needs.
- What changes have happened to the important and teachable people in your life that may result in changes to your relationship with them? What should be your response to such changes? Be sure to include family members in this exercise.
- What information have you been focusing on? How can you change your information focus so you can develop, grow and improve your effectiveness in the world around you? You may want to briefly examine your subject list and filing index.

  Once you have collected these thoughts, refer to the appropriate templates, and take time to:

- Redefine your roles using adjectives
- Relate appropriate goals to your roles. Make sure they are SMART goals
- Update your people inventory focusing on the important and teachable people
- Communicate with the important people to ensure that they agree with you and support you in your redefined roles and goals
- Examine your mission statement and make appropriate changes, if needed
- Mark a time in future when you again plan to maintain your filtering system

Your filing system is an infrastructure to support you in fulfilling your roles and achieving your goals. The frequency of its maintenance requirements depends on your roles. The following are some thoughts and tips to guide you:

Maintaining your INBOX

Your information input handling protocols define the responsiveness and inbox processing commitments you made.

This will help you maintain your inboxes. If you have committed to a well-balanced communication protocol and are exercising batch processing, your inbox will automatically be maintained.

Periodically, especially if you have experienced changes in your roles and goals, you may find it necessary to adjust your communication and inbox handling protocol. This should include your e-mail, phone, meetings, and paper handling protocol.

Here are some questions to help you think through such changes:

- Examine the inbox handling section of your Overload gauge and identify areas of possible need. What changes can you make to reduce the overload factor?
- Are your important people pleased with your communication level and quality? Take time to ask them.
- What changes do you need to make to your personal inbox handling protocol?

Note: Your briefcase should be maintained daily or every time you need to use it.

Maintaining your HOT FILE:

Your HOT FILE holds the information you need most frequently. It needs to be simple, crisp, and clean. The following may help you maintain this file:

- Examine the filing section of your information overload gauge and identify areas of possible need. What changes can you make to reduce the overload factor?
- Examine the contents of the HOT FILE and move any files you no longer need to the reference or archive sections.
- Where appropriate, discard, delete or donate any unwanted material.

- What is the best frequency of maintaining this file? Mark this in your calendar as a regularly scheduled appointment with yourself. We recommend that you consider this as a **weekly maintenance plan**.

Maintaining your REFERENCE File:

Your reference file holds the information you need less frequently. The following may help you maintain this file:

- Examine the contents of the reference file and move any material that is not needed to the archive sections.
- Where appropriate, discard, delete or donate any unwanted material.
- What is the best frequency of maintaining this file? Mark this in your calendar as a regularly scheduled appointment with yourself. We recommend that you consider this as a **monthly maintenance plan.**

Maintaining your ARCHIVE File:

Your ARCHIVE FILE holds the information you may never need. The following may help maintain this file:

- Examine the contents of the ARCHIVE FILE and discard any material that is not needed.
- Where appropriate, discard, delete, or donate any unwanted material.
- What is the best frequency of maintaining this file? Mark this in your calendar as a regularly scheduled appointment with yourself. We recommend that you consider this as an **annual maintenance plan**.

Maintaining your DELETE File:

Your DELETE file holds the information you hope you will never need but are not ready to discard. The following may help maintain this file:

- How is the delete or computer recycle bin parameter set up? Can you set similar parameters for your paper delete files?
- What is a reasonable retention plan for such a file? We recommend that you consider three months as a reasonable period.

Exercise:

Using the following table, write what you believe is a reasonable maintenance schedule for your system. Commit to regular frequency and mark it in your calendar

System To Be Maintained and Commitment: I will maintain my: **Daily, Weekly, Monthly Or Annually ↘**	**Frequency**	**When?**
☐ **Filtering System** (Roles, Goals, and Important People List)		
☐ **Mission Statement**		
☐ **Personal Communication Protocol** (For e-mail, phone, paper, and meetings including the e-mail filtering rules)		
☐ **Inbox** (Allowing enough time to batch process e-mail, phone calls, paper, and the thoughts that result from meetings and other input.)		
☐ **HOT FILE** (e-mail, paper, and hard drive)		
☐ **REFERENCE FILE** (e-mail, paper, and hard drive)		
☐ **ARCHIVE FILE** (paper and hard drive assuming e-mail archive will be controlled by auto-archiving function)		
☐ **DELETE FILE** (paper and hard drive assuming e-mail will be controlled by its own system)		

Summary:

- ✓ If not maintained, all systems deteriorate into decay and become more burdensome than useful.
- ✓ Maintaining your filtering system will help you identify changes to your roles and goals in response to your changing world.
- ✓ Maintaining your INBOX based on your communication protocols will help ensure your communication commitments to your important people.
- ✓ Maintaining your HOT FILE on a weekly basis will reduce the clutter and keep this file crisp and clean. This will enable you to find what you need quickly, reducing the time wasted in searching for information when you need it.
- ✓ Maintaining your REFERENCE FILE on a monthly basis will keep it organized and accessible for you and others without too much difficulty.
- ✓ Maintaining your ARCHIVE FILE annually will keep it organized and accessible for you and others without too much difficulty. In addition, weeding this file aggressively will significantly reduce your filing requirements and save you much valuable office space.
- ✓ Maintaining your DELETE FILE monthly will help you reduce the clutter without much risk. The originator of documents should retain copies of what they create and should be willing to provide you with copies, if you do not have one.
- ✓ Your briefcase should be maintained daily or every time you need to use it.

PART FIVE:

IF IT'S TO BE, IT'S UP TO ME

- Your Personal Action Plan
- If You Want to Be a Master of an Art, Coach It
- Coaching Through Delegation
- Coaching Tools
  - Templates
  - Discussion Questions

Part Five – If It's to Be, It's up To Me

What Is Your Action Plan? Do You Want To Help Others? *As you develop your personal action plan you can also be a good coach and have a great influence. Becoming a good coach can help you improve your skills while helping others in overcoming overload.*

16 – Your Personal Action Plan

Today most leaders and knowledge workers feel overloaded. The Personal Knowledge Management Framework is a solution that you can personally tailor in response to your needs. This solution is designed to help you change, if you choose to. Yes, to a very great part, change is a personal choice.

Motivated by the promise of more effective living and concerns for the negative impact of overload, many of our workshop participants have chosen to change. Our hope is that you will choose to exchange your overloaded world for one that is more effective and balanced.

Nothing will change unless you take the first step and have an action plan. Overcoming overload in an overloaded world is not easy. By nature, we easily surrender to bad habits. In an overloaded world, good behaviors are often counter culture. You will likely face opposition from draining people who have often contributed to your overloaded world. You will be tempted to avoid the efforts and discipline that lead to improved effectiveness and a balanced life.

A reasonable action plan is a statement of faith and commitment. You must have faith and believe that you are embarking on a valuable endeavor that has positive consequences. You must be committed to reasonable discipline and changed behavior. Towards this goal, you must be supported by your important people who encourage you and who may hold you accountable for doing what you want to do.

My advice to an overloaded person trying to address the problem is to be determined but also patient with themselves. The required behaviors to address overload are counter-culture to most of the work world today, and one can expect to face some resistance that may shake one's confidence. Therefore the change will take time and determination and patience are both required so that one does not give up in frustration.

Mr. Doug Stirling, Director of Corporate Accounting

<u>TIP:</u> What Can You Do?

Examine the **Personal Knowledge Management Framework** illustrated in Diagram 3 below and decide which two frames you want to focus on right now. Later, you can focus on other frames. For now, we encourage you to focus on only two frames. You may make your choice based on the frames that:

- You find most interesting or
- Are likely to bring you the greatest benefits or
- Are the easiest to implement

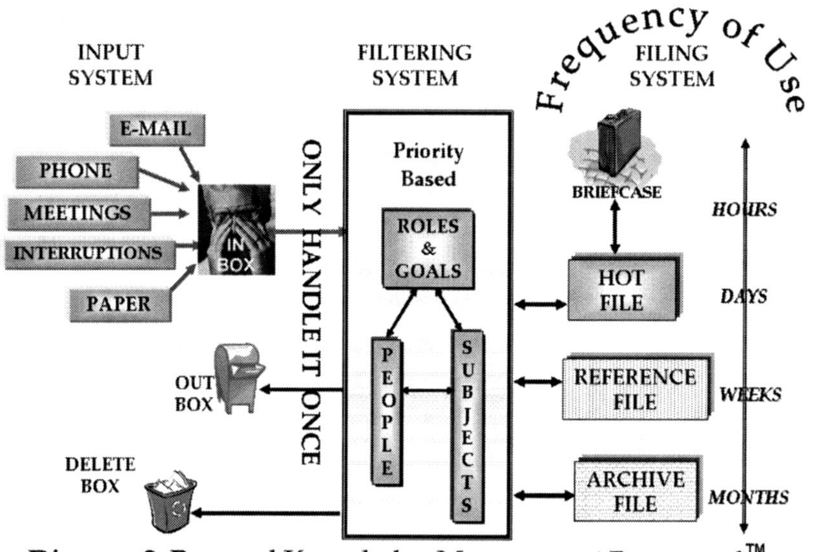

Diagram 3: Personal Knowledge Management Framework™

For each of your chosen two frames write the reason why you have chosen them and the benefits you expect to get from focusing on them or the changes you will start to make. Then write SMART goals using the simple goal development templates that we discussed in chapter 4. If you need to, refer to the chapters that relate to the frames on which you are focusing. It will help you to record how you will be held accountable for accomplishing your goals.

Exercise:

Using the following table, write your personal action plan

The First Frame I will focus on is:		
The reason I am focusing on this frame is:		
SMART Goal – What? What do I want to happen? (Accomplishment)	**How?** How will I know it happened? (Actions)	**By When?** Target date
For Accountability I will		

The Second Frame I will focus on is:		
The reason I am focusing on this frame is:		
SMART Goal – What? What do I want to happen? (Accomplishment)	**How?** How will I know it happened? (Actions)	**By When?** Target date
For Accountability I will		

I lead a very large multi-facility organization. I carry a very responsible job. At the same time, everybody around me knows that I am very active in my family life and very supportive of community involvement. This is not hard to do when you set the right priorities and communicate them.

My advice to a young professional is: Take note. You will find yourself in your fifties a lot sooner than you think, so pace yourself. There is more to life than money and work. The things you are giving up now to earn the big bucks cannot be recovered.

Mr. John McGarry, President and Chief Executive Officer

17 – If You Want to Be a Master of an Art, Coach It

If you have found any of the material in this book helpful, you have an opportunity to master these skills by becoming a coach and helping someone else.

- ✓ Do you know any overloaded people?
- ✓ Do you care about the stress of your coworkers, neighbors, and business associates?
- ✓ Are there any individuals around your workplace that you feel can benefit from the material you have just learned?
- ✓ Have you had any experiences that you believe can help others improve their effectiveness and reverse the negative impact of overload?

If you answered yes to any of the above questions, you have a unique opportunity to gain great rewards while helping someone else. You can enhance your overload management skills while at the same time making a positive impact on the world around you. Yes, you can be someone's coach.

You are a coach. Being a coach is one of the most rewarding of life experiences. Intentionally or unintentionally, directly or indirectly, we all are coaches. We all lead and influence others by our example as well as by our words. As people observe your changed behavior, and hopefully the positive outcome that you have gained, they will be curious and receptive to your counsel and encouragement.

To help us change work habits that contribute to overload as a management team we introduced a buddy system. I have a buddy. We meet regularly, discuss overload challenges and progress, as well as hold each other accountable for disciplines to which we commit.

Ms. Donna Johnston, People Manager

A coach is not a person who is able to do something better than his or her protégé. A good coach is one who is able to help his or her protégé do things better. While the ultimate beneficiary of coaching is the protégé, impacting lives for good energizes you as you see the positive impact you have on the lives of others. Effective coaching is based on:

1. **Convictions and shared values**: It is critical that your coaching be based on personal conviction in what you believe is best. Such values must be shared and accepted by your protégé in absolute honesty.
2. **Commitment to disciplined accountability:** Coaching has a cost. You must agree with your protégé that there is a price to be paid by each of you. Your payment is in terms of time and commitment to his or her progress. Your protégé pays in terms of discipline and accountability, and a sincere desire for **visible and changed behavior**.
3. **Clear communication:** Clarity of communication is essential for good coaching. While verbal communication and body language are essential, the use of written communication serves for ongoing reference and confirmation of agreements.
4. **Honesty and integrity:** A coach is not perfect. An honest coach admits failures and expresses opinions with integrity. Sharing your experiences and struggles with integrity is critical to your successful coaching efforts. At the same time your protégé must admit the need for help and commit to progress, not perfection.

Over the years I have experienced and observed good leaders and poor leaders. Good leaders focus on inspiring, developing, and coaching people The highest responsibility of leaders is to create more leaders through coaching. Coaching people instills confidence and self esteem in people. A quote I read one time said, "We teach what we need to learn ourselves." Coaching has dual benefits. When I coach someone I learn greatly through the process. You cannot be a coach or mentor and not be a student at the same time. This multiplies the benefits of the coaching experience. Leadership is all about people.

Ms. Karen MacDonald, Regional Director, Quality Improvement and Education

Coaching is a critical management skill. Organizational development hinges on developing a coaching culture. I am a teacher at heart. I know that a subject like overcoming overload requires changed behavior. You cannot expect people to change by simply sending them on a course or have them listen to a lecture. Coaching enforces the learned disciplines required for changed behavior.

Coaching brings great benefits to the managers as well as the staff they coach. In our organization we instituted a new buddy system. Senior staff is given a lower workload and are assigned coaching responsibilities for which they are accountable.

Ms. Pat Clinch, Director Organizational Development

TIPS: What can you do? Commit to teachable people.

1. Make a list of your teachable people and identify the ones you believe respect you and admire your behaviour. Engage them as individuals by:
   a. Asking them how they feel about the overloaded world in which we live
   b. Sharing with them your experience and what you are doing to overcome overload
   c. Offering to meet with them on a regular basis and work through some of these issues. If they agree, define your next meeting time and place. Provide them with a copy of the **Information Anxiety Syndrome** template and the **Information Overload Gauge** template. If they can afford it, have them purchase their own copy of **"Overloaded?"** This will provide lots of content for discussion and applications.
2. In your next meeting, using the **Overload Gauge**, identify the areas that deserve the most attention and those on which your protégé wants to work. Help your protégé document an action plan. Agree on:
   a. Meeting regularly to review and discuss progress
   b. How often you will meet (weekly, bi-weekly or monthly)

c. How much time you will spend in each meeting (no more than 1 hour)
d. How long the term of your coaching agreement will be (three to six months)
e. How you will disengage from this agreement should life circumstances lead to changed priorities and/or if progress is not realized

3. Support your protégé with gentleness and accountability.

18 – Coaching by Delegation. Delegate Roles, Not Tasks

As you coach individuals, they appreciate your interest and life investments in them. They become very loyal to you and more desirous of paying back by helping you in return. This is your chance to leverage this relationship and to take the next step that could bring great rewards for you and for your protégé.

When it comes to delegation, most of us think of delegating tasks. We delegate tasks we do not like. Most of us delegate for the purpose of reducing our burden and getting rid of unpleasant chores. Here we encourage you to **delegate roles, not tasks.** We encourage you to delegate for the purpose of helping your protégé grow and develop as you focus on higher value roles.

For example, supposing that as a committee member you receive an e-mail with a long report attached to it. As you examine its subject you recall that one of your teachable people is interested in that subject matter. Forward that e-mail to your protégé asking him or her to study it and discuss any relevant content during a one on one time that you spend.

This one on one time your spend with your protégé will become not only a learning time for you but more importantly a coaching time that will help your protégé grow through this experience. You may be able to even go a step further by delegating your role on that committee to your protégé freeing you even more precious time.

TIP: What Can You Do?

As you focus on higher value roles, goals, and activities, you must give up lower value roles, goals, and activities. Examine the various roles you play. Identify areas you are prepared to delegate to your protégé in a manner that can help him or her grow. For example, suppose you are a member of a certain operational committee and you wish to devote more time to leadership and coaching roles. Select one of your protégés whom you think can benefit from the management exposure and delegate your role on that committee. In doing so be careful:

- To ensure that your protégé has the time to assume his or her new role with competence
- To encourage your protégé to rehearse their role and bring added value to the role using his or her own distinctive views, skills, and talents
- To make sure that all others understand that your protégé is in charge and has your full confidence and support and that you will not get involved unless your protégé asks for help
- To let your protégé learn from failure and mistakes. It is always tempting for you to try to help. Remember, **"During the game the coach should not get on the field of play."**

Effective delegation is never abdication. Never delegate to avoid responsibility or negative outcome. Effective delegation carefully considers the learning needs and ability of the person to whom you are delegating. Take lots of time to communicate all expectations, timelines, process, and authority. Be sure you are able to provide appropriate feedback and support as well as needed authority. Delegation often takes more work than doing something yourself but it is critical for the growth of the intellectual capital of an organization.

Ms. Susan Malenica, Regional Director

Effective delegation takes time, requires planning and clarity in communication by the delegator. It also requires follow-up support and encouragement. When delegating we make two common mistakes. The first is that we often quickly delegate prescribed tasks rather than carefully communicating the role that we are delegating.

Delegating roles allows the protégé more latitude in using their judgment, and in the end brings greater development and a sense of achievement.

The second common mistake is that we treat people like a "fire-and-forget missile". We hand it to them and forget it, leaving them perhaps to flounder on difficult issues. It is important to be available to the Protégé to provide a regular point of support and encouragement. This is the reason why effective delegation and coaching go hand in hand.

Mr. Doug Stirling, Director of Corporate Accounting

We are a sports family. Without good coaches my children would not have progressed as they did in their highly demanding sports. It is the same in life. Having a good coach is a most valuable asset.

In the absence of coaching we must learn through personal experience often repeating the same mistakes several times before we discover the solution. Coaching enforces the positive while at the same time bringing an honest, objective external set of eyes to help you see the negative and define what needs to change. The priority of a good coach centers on the development of the individual without necessarily having a vested interest in the expected action or outcome.

Ms. Andrea Seymour, Vice President and Chief Information Officer

Summary:

- ✓ We all coach and influence others by our example, words, and habits.
- ✓ Overload is a prevailing problem in our society. This offers a unique opportunity for coaching and developing your skills while helping others as well.
- ✓ Successful coaching is based on convictions, shared values, commitment to disciplined accountability, clear communication, honesty, and integrity.
- ✓ Coach teachable people who respect you and are prepared to enter into a disciplined coaching agreement with you.
- ✓ Use the **Information Anxiety** template and the **Information Overload Gauge** template to define coaching objectives.
- ✓ Use this resource book as a tool to provide discussion material and to help you establish a coaching plan.
- ✓ Coach through delegation. This will help you develop your protégé and free your valuable resources enabling you to focus on higher value roles, goals, and activities.

19 – Coaching Tools, Templates, and Discussion Questions

Templates are tools to help you write your thoughts so you can see them and share them with others. The objectives of these templates are to:

- Provide simple structures or a process to guide your thinking and/or your discussions as you coach your protégé
- Provide a reference point to help you keep discussions on track and avoid distractions or going off on tangents
- Provide a forum of clear accountability ensuring coaching commitments and discipline are maintained
- Offer a yardstick to gauge progress and reward success

Templates

Our templates are flexible, so use what we provide as an example and create your own templates to fit your needs and personal style. In the following highlights we reference the Chapter number where you can see an example of the template as well as more detail about the applications.

Information Anxiety Symptoms - Chapter 1

- **Purpose:** This is **NOT** a clinical assessment tool. The purpose of this template is to help you and/or your protégé focus and prioritize the most critical symptoms of information and work overload.
- **Entry descriptions / actions:** Examine each symptom; identify the most pressing ones based on the frequency of how often you feel that way. Try to focus only on three most critical symptoms. As you progress in dealing with the overload problem, refer to this symptoms list often.

Overload Gauge - Chapter 1

- **Purpose:** This gauge is not intended to be a scientific measurement. It is designed to help you understand how you identify the most critical causes of information and work overload. These are broken into three categories that relate to the solutions provided in the **Personal Knowledge Management Framework**. The first group of statements deals with the importance of setting priorities based on important roles, goals, and subjects. The second deals with the sources of information input. The third deals with the filing system.
- **Entry descriptions/ actions:** Indicate to what extent you agree or disagree with each statement. Do not be overly analytical. Your first impression is the most important. Add the score of each group as well the total for all four groups combined. Identify which group of the gauge, and where appropriate which frame, deserves the most attention. Once this is carefully examined, it serves as a springboard towards developing an action plan. Later you can use the scores as a yardstick to frequently assess progress.

Template A – Roles Inventory - Chapter 3

- **Purpose***:* This template serves to help you list, prioritize, and describe the high value roles on which you and/or your protégé need to focus. Once written, these roles and their related descriptions can be discussed and negotiated with others.
- **Entry descriptions/ actions***:* Think of and list all your important roles. Try to group them into leadership roles, project roles, and operational roles. Further, you may wish to consider them in light of personal, family, business, and community related roles. If you find that you have too many roles listed, identify the most important five in each category. Describe each role using the most appropriate adjectives. If you have too many adjectives, highlight the most important adjectives. Your important people will help you to define your roles. Take time seeking their input or

comparing their perception of your roles and how they describe them. Negotiate with them for the most appropriate description.

Template B – Goals Inventory - Chapter 4

- **Purpose:** The objective is to write **SMART** goals that relate to the high value roles you identified in Template A. **SMART** goals are Specific, Measurable, Agreed upon, Realistic and Time dependant.
- **Entry descriptions/ actions:** For each role list the **accomplishment** or what you need to see happen. Write the step-by-step activities that you need to undertake to achieve each accomplishment. Start each activity using an active verb. Do not forget to write your completion target date. Most actions require time. To ensure that actions are carried out, we recommend that they be recorded in your calendar or time management system.

Template C – People Inventory - Chapter 5

- **Purpose:** This template is to help you prioritize the people in your life. The outcome is a prioritized list of names that should relate to your roles and to your time investment.
- **Entry descriptions/ actions:** Using whatever sources you choose, examine your contact list. Code these names as I = Important, T = Teachable and D = Draining. Transcribe these onto your template. In some cases one name may have more than one code (I, T, D). Write your reason for that assessment or importance. Relate these names to the important roles they play in your life or the important roles you play in their lives.

Template D – Subjects Inventory - Chapter 6

- **Purpose:** The objective is to develop a filing index of the information subjects that are important to the fulfillment of your roles. This should help reduce information clutter as well as facilitating filing and information retrieval.
- **Entry descriptions/ actions:** List subjects and sub subjects. Where appropriate, relate each entry to the role or roles they impact.

Filter at a Glance- Chapter 6

- **Purpose:** The objective is to provide a summary that can be easily referred to and often updated. This is a tool by which you can make easy and quick filtering decisions.
- **Entry descriptions/ actions:** List your most important roles. For each role list your most important goals or accomplishment you want to see happen within a reasonable time period. List the names or initials of the most important people that impact or will be impacted by that role. List the most important subjects that relate to that role and/or the information you need to collect to help you fulfill that role or achieve that goal.

Template E – Communication and Note Taking Sheet - Chapter 10

- **Purpose:** The objective is to provide **one place** to capture all notes, thoughts, interactions, and related responses.
- **Entry descriptions/ actions:** At the beginning of a day record the day and date. As the day progresses write details appropriate for each encounter, communication, or thought. Include the time and type of communication. Record the source and appropriate thought. If a response is requested or received, indicate this as well. If delegation is needed, record to whom the matter is delegated and target due date. To help you prioritize your focus or needed follow- up indicate the ABC priorities, if you wish. Periodically, say once a month, staple all the sheets used in this period and file them away as a communication and notes record.

  If you are taking notes in a meeting, the top part of this sheet provides a space to record the meeting title, meeting location and the meeting attendees. At the end of your meeting, if you need to, file related sheets in an appropriate file with the meeting title. Review your notes against the meeting minutes when they arrive.

Template F– VIP– Thoughts and Tips - Chapter 11

- **Purpose:** The objectives are to reduce interruptions and distractions by sorting and batch processing thoughts related to **one person** and to provide an agenda or a list of points for future discussion.
- **Entry descriptions/ actions:** This template is similar in layout to Template E. Write the name of the person with whom you plan to communicate. As required, record the date and your thoughts. You may choose to record the priority of the item in question as A, B or C. When the time comes to discuss the point in question, write the response in the response section. For a historical record, file these sheets in a folder labeled with the name of the person.

Template G – Supplies List - Chapter 14

- **Purpose:** The objective is to ensure that you have all the supplies needed for optimum operational efficiency.
- **Entry descriptions/ actions:** Examine your office supplies and mark what you need before going shopping or placing an order for the needed supplies. Repeat this process periodically.

Template H: Meeting Effectiveness Analysis – Chapter 10

- **Purpose:** The objective is to assess the effective use or your meeting participation.

Entry descriptions/ actions: Using any average week examine your calendar recording the total hours spent in meetings including preparation, travel, and follow-up. **"Guestimate"** your effectiveness ratio and your wasted time for that week. Your wasted life value is double the wasted time as it reflects the wasted time plus the wasted opportunity cost.

Discussion Questions

Questions are more powerful than opinions in developing a coaching forum. As you seek to interact with others you may find that asking the right question is essential for starting the dialogue and keeping your interaction on track. The following questions could be of help to:

- Individuals seeking to coach others towards a more effective and balanced life
- Leaders as they seek to interact with their teams in uncovering causes and symptoms, as well as solutions to the overload problem

These questions are provided in a topical manner that relates to the sections and chapters provided in this book. You may find it helpful to refer to the related chapters. You may also find it helpful to use the templates provided in some chapters as a way of documenting your interactions and discussion.

PART 1: STATE OF THE KNOWLEDGE WORKER –

(Refer to Chapters 1 & 2)

1. Do believe that you are overloaded? Why?
2. What is the picture that comes to your mind when you hear the term "overload"?
3. What are the key contributors to overload in your business environment?
4. What are the key contributors to overload in your personal life?
5. How does the corporate culture positively or negatively impact the overload problem?
6. How does information technology positively or negatively impact the overload problem?
7. How does the supply and demand for talent have a positive or negative impact on the overload problem in your professional field?

8. In your work environment, what positive indicators offer hope for those who seek to change their overloaded world?

PART 2: FILTERING, KEEPING OVERLOAD AT BAY

Filtering on High Value Roles: (Refer to Chapter 3)

9. What are the most important roles on which you like to focus? Why?
10. What are the most important adjectives that describe these roles?
11. To what extent do your important people understand and support the roles you want to focus on?
12. What percentage of your time is spent on the Leadership, Project, and Operational Stages?
13. Examining your important roles, what should be the optimum mix of the time you spend on the Leadership, Project, and Operational Stages?

Filtering on High Value Goals (Refer to Chapter 4)

14. What are the SMART goals that relate to your important roles? Are they documented?
15. What are the accomplishments you want to see and the activities you need to do to achieve these goals?
16. To what extent do your important people understand and support your goals?
17. What accountability forum do you have to help keep your commitment towards achieving your important goals?

Filtering on High Value Relationships (Refer to Chapter 5)

18. Who are the important people who help you define your roles and are critical to the achievement of your goals?
19. To what extent do your important people appreciate and agree to the **role they play in your life?**
20. As you examine your calendar what changes do you need to make to enhance your relationship with your important people?

21. Whom do you identify as your teachable people?

22. To what extent do your teachable people appreciate and agree on the **role you play in their life?**

23. As you examine your calendar, what changes do you need to make to enhance the impact you make on your teachable people?

Filtering on High Value Subjects (Refer to Chapter 6)

24. How is your life driven by urgent and important matters? Why?

25. Who are the sources of your urgent, emotionally draining subjects?

26. Who presents you with the important, thought provoking subjects?

27. Does your information filing system help you be more proactive or leave you victim to the urgency driven world?

Have a Mission Statement (Refer to Chapter 7)

28. What would you say if asked, "What is your purpose for living?"

29. How does your personal mission statement relate to your important and teachable people?

30. To what extent does the mission statement of the corporation you work for or the associations to which you belong reflect your passion and commitments?

31. If you were to develop a "modified **corporate** mission statement" that better reflects your roles, goals, and activities in that corporation or association, what would that mission statement say?

PART 3: OVERCOMING THE SOURCES OF OVERLOAD

Overcoming E-Mail Overload (Refer to Chapter 8)

32. When does e-mail become a cause for overload in your life?

33. What are the reasonable e-mail responsiveness expectations for your important roles?

34. How can you best communicate a reasonable e-mail protocol to your important people?
35. How can you batch process your e-mail at regular time intervals in keeping with the responsiveness you established?
36. How can you best use the rules filtering tool to prioritize your incoming e-mail?

Overcoming Telephone Overload (Refer to Chapter 9)

37. When does the phone become a cause for overload in your life?
38. What are the phone call return expectations for the important roles you play?
39. What is the best outgoing voice message that you can use to set reasonable expectations on the part of your callers?
40. How can you batch process your voice mail at regular time intervals?
41. How do you set objectives and goals for your calls before engaging in them to make your calls more effective?

Overcoming Meeting Overload (Refer to Chapter 10)

42. In your organization to what extent do you waste time in meetings?
43. Considering your high value roles, what percentage of your workday should you spend in meetings? How does this compare with your present state? Be sure to include meeting preparation, travel, and follow-up time as well as electronic meetings and long phone calls.
44. How can you schedule time to process all the input you receive during critical meetings?
45. What changes can you make to ensure that your meeting participation delivers higher value to you and those who attend?
46. If you lead meetings, what changes can you make to ensure that you deliver higher value to all who attend?

Overcoming Interruptions (Refer to Chapter 11)

47. How do interruptions impact your productivity?
48. How do interruptions from phone calls, e-mail, instant messaging and unscheduled meetings impact your emotions?
49. How can you limit instant messaging access and those who view your availability?
50. How can you batch process e-mail and voice mail to reduce interruptions?
51. How can you use the VIP sheet described in Chapter 11 to reduce personal interruptions?
52. What disciplines can you place to control self imposed interruptions that reduce your effectiveness?

Overcoming Paper Overload (Refer to Chapter 12)

53. To what extent has the electronic world had a positive or negative impact on the use of paper in your office?
54. What is the source of your important paper mail and how can you reduce its clutter?
55. What can you do to reduce paper clutter in your office?

PART 4: DEVELOPING A CLUTTER FREE FILING SYSTEM (Refer to Chapter 13)

56. What do you think of the **"Frequency of Use Filing Methodology"?**
57. Are there practical, common subject headings that can be used by most of your team?
58. What is the best layout or location for the HOT, REFERENCE, and ARCHIVE FILES?
59. Would it be helpful to have common departmental REFERENCE And/Or ARCHIVE FILES? How can they be best maintained?
60. What document retention guidelines can best support your important roles? Can you establish common document retention guidelines for your team?

61. How can you apply common filing structures to the paper, e-mail, and electronic files?

Building a Clutter Free Filing System (Refer to Chapter 14)

62. Can you arrange a common teamwork effort to reduce office clutter?
63. Can you arrange your own work period to get the paper, electronic and/or e-mail files organized?
64. What accountability measures can help fulfill the commitment to organize your files?
65. Can a common supplies room be helpful? Who will maintain it?

Maintaining a Clutter Free Filing System

(Refer to Chapter 15)

66. What is a practical maintenance plan for your filtering system?
67. What is a practical maintenance plan for your filing system?
68. Would it be practical to have a departmental maintenance plan?

PART 5: IF IT'S TO BE, IT'S UP TO ME

Your Personal Action Plan (Refer to Chapter 16)

69. Examining the topics presented by the **Personal Knowledge Management Framework** which frames will bring you the greatest benefits and why?
70. What do you want to see accomplished in the next eight weeks and what activities will you undertake to achieve this?
71. How will you ensure that you will follow through with your plan and what accountability will you put in place?

If You Want to Be a Master of an Art, Coach It

(Refer to Chapter 17)

72. Can you name two people that you would like to coach or you are coaching today that can benefit from improved work/life balance?

73. What are the objectives you would like to accomplish from your coaching experience?
74. What plans have you and your protégés agreed on that will ensure you reach your coaching objectives?
75. Are your objectives and plans written and regularly reviewed with your protégés?

Coaching by Delegation. Delegate Roles, Not Tasks (Refer To Chapter 18)

76. Do you have a list of the roles that you plan to delegate to your teachable people?
77. Have you communicated to your protégés that you empower them and expect them to bring their own distinctive to the roles you delegate to them?
78. Have you clearly defined your role as a coach to your protégés?

Coaching Tools, Templates and Discussion Questions (Refer to Chapter 19)

79. What tools do you presently use to clearly communicate your coaching plans? Can these be enhanced?
80. What tools do you presently use to communicate accountability in your relationships with your protégés? Can these be enhanced?

ENDNOTES

Part One

[1] Richard A. Swenson, *The Overload Syndrome: Learning to Live within Your Limits* (Colorado Springs, Colorado: Navpress, 1998), page 135.

[2] Francis Narin, "Tech-Line Background Paper 3. Research Background."
http://www.chiresearch.com/docs/tlbp.pdf (17 July 2004).

[3] http://www.census.gov (11June 2004). (Several tables are used for U.S. Census Bureau population figures.)

[4] Eric Beauchesne, "Skilled Labor Shortage Nearing, Study Says," *National Post,* 10 July 2002, section A, page 3.

[5] Tony Seskus, "Skilled Help Shortage Hits Canada," *National Post,* 30 December 2002, section FP, page 1.

[6]"How Much Information? 2003."
http://www.sims.berkeley.edu/research/projects/how-much-info-2003/execsum.htm#summary (11June 2004).

[7] Wayne J. Hunicke, "Improving the Quality of Your Meetings."
http://www.advantagemgmt.com/resource/meetings.html (5 July 2004).

[8] Richard A. Swenson, *The Overload Syndrome: Learning to Live within Your Limits* (Colorado Springs, Colorado: Navpress, 1998), page 138.

[9] "E-Mail Leads Workers to Use 40% More Paper, Study Says," *National Post,* 19 November 2001, section D, page 1.

[10] "How Much Information? 2003"
http://www.sims.berkeley.edu/research/projects/how-much-info-2003/execsum.htm#summary (11June 2004).

[11] John B. Izzo and Pam Withers, *Values Shift: The New Work Ethic and What It Means for Business* (Toronto: Prentice Hall Canada), page 79.

Part Two

[12] William Shakespeare, *As You Like It* (New York: Simon & Schuster, 1959), II, vii, 149.

[13] Gordon Macdonald, *Restoring Your Spiritual Passion* (Nashville: Thomas Nelson, 1986).

[14] Stephen R. Covey, *The Seven Habits of Highly Effective People: Restoring the Character Ethic* (New York: Simon and Schuster, 1989).

[15] Charles E. Hummel, *Tyranny of the Urgent* (Downers Grove, Illinois: InterVarsity Press, 1967), page 5.

[16] Merrill E. and Donna N. Douglass, *Manage Your Time Your Work Yourself: The Updated Edition* (New York: AMACOM, 1993), page 26.

[17] Edward R. Dayton and Ted W. Engstrom, *Strategy for Living* (Glendale, California: G/L Publications, 1976), page 67.

[18] Edward R. Dayton and Ted W. Engstrom, *Strategy for Living* (Glendale, California: G/L Publications, 1976).

Part Three

[19] Jaroslav Pelikan, ed., *Luther's Works*. Volume 21. (Saint Louis: Concordia Publishing House, 1956), page 88.

[20] Christopher Saunders, "Study: E-mail to Double by 2006." http://www.clickz.com/news/article.php/1471801 (5 July 2004).

[21] Nancy Flynn and Randolph Kahn, *E-Mail Rules: A Business Guide to Managing Policies, Security, and Legal*

Issues, for E-Mail and Digital Communications (New York: AMACOM, 2003), page 12.

[22] Kaitlin Duck Sherwood, "Tips for Overcoming Email Overload." http://www.overcomeemailoverload.com/advice/TopTenTips.html (11 June 2004).

[23] Gihan Perera, "Ten Tips for Filing Your E-Mail." http://www.firststep.com.au/articles/filing-email.html (5 November 2001).

[24] "Several Answers about Managing E-Mail." http://www.tmius.com/4tmcorn.HTML (5 November 2001).

[25] "E-mail." http://www.witc.tec.wi.us/library/tips/nrich/internet.htm#email (5 November 2001).

[26] Ellen Roseman, "Staying on Top of Your Virtual World," *Toronto Star*, 22 February 2004, section C, page 1.

[27] Harold Taylor, "Don't Let E-mail Ruin Communications," *Mississauga Business Times*, July 2001, page 34.

[28] Ann Massie Nelson, "Voice Mail Puts Onus on Lawyer to Respond." http://www.wisbar.org/wislawmag/1997/09/risk.html (18 October 2001).

[29] Laura M. Stack, "Taming the Telephone." http://www.theproductivitypro.com/newsletters/newsletter10.htm (15 January 2002).

[30] Laura M. Stack, "Voice Mail Tips." http://www.theproductivitypro.com/newsletters/Number%202%20March%201999.htm (16 June 2004).

[31] A network MCI Conferencing White Paper. Meetings in America: A Study of Trends, Costs and Attitudes toward Business Travel, Teleconferencing, and Their Impact on Productivity (Greenwich, CT: INFOCOMM, 1998), page 3.

[32]Wayne J. Hunicke, "Improving the Quality of Your Meetings." http://www.advantagemgmt.com/resource/meetings.html (5 July 2004).

[33] Ibid.

[34] "Getting the Most out of Meetings." http://www.mindtools.com/tmmeetng.html (16 June 2004).

[35] Laura M. Stack, "Meetings! Where Minutes Are Kept and Hours Wasted." http://www.theproductivitypro.com/newsletters/num61June2004.htm (16 June 2004).

[36] Lorraine Weygman, "'Energize' Your Meetings So They Don't Waste Time…" *North York Business News,* January 1989.

[37] Patricia Pickett, "Interruptions Reduce Staff Productivity," *ComputerWorld Canada,* 5 September 2003, page 25.

[38] Laura M. Stack, "Dealing with Interruptions from Visitors." http://www.theproductivitypro.com/newsletters/Number%204%20June%201999.htm (16 June 2004).

[39] "E-Mail Leads Workers to Use 40% More Paper, Study Says," *National Post,* 19 November 2001, section D, page 1.

[40] Kathryn Alesandrini, *Survive Information Overload: The 7 Best Ways to Manage Your Workload by Seeing the Big Picture* (Homewood, Illinois: Business One Irwin, 1992) page 71.

[41] Christina Cavanagh, *Managing Your E-Mail: Thinking outside the Inbox*. (Hoboken, New Jersey: John Wiley & Sons, 2003) page 34.

[42] Susan Felding, "The High Cost of Not Finding Information," *Kmworld*, March 2004, page 9.

[43] Paul Waddington, "Dying for Information? A Report on the Effects of Information Overload in the UK and Worldwide." http://www.cni.org/regconfs/1997/ukoln-content/repor~13.html (3 October 2001).

[44] Susan Silver, *Organized to Be Your Best! Simplify and Improve How You Work* ([Los Angeles]: Adams-Hall Publishing, 2000), page 105.

[45] Stephanie Winston, *The Organized Executive: The Classic Program for Productivity: New Ways to Manage Time, Paper, People, and the Digital Office* (New York: Warner Books, 2001), page 103.

[46] Ibid, page 92.

[47] Frank Steiger, "The Second Law of Thermodynamics, Evolution and Probability." http://www.talkorigins.org/faqs/thermo/probability.html (22 June 2004).

BIBLIOGRAPHY

BOOKS

Alesandrini, Kathryn. *Survive Information Overload: The 7 Best Ways to Manage Your Workload by Seeing the Big Picture*. Homewood, Illinois: Business One Irwin, 1992.

Burleson, Clyde W. *Effective Meetings: The Complete Guide*. New York: John Wiley & Sons, 1990.

Butler, Ava S. *Team Think: 72 Ways to Make Good, Smart, Quick Decisions in Any Meeting*. New York: McGraw-Hill, 1996.

Caunt, John. *30 Minutes ... to Manage Information Overload*. London: Kogan Page, 1999.

Cavanagh, Christina. *Managing Your E-Mail: Thinking outside the Inbox*. Hoboken, New Jersey: John Wiley & Sons, 2003.

Covey, Stephen R. *The Seven Habits of Highly Effective People: Restoring the Character Ethic*. New York: Simon & Schuster, 1989.

Dayton, Edward R. and Ted W. Engstrom. *Strategy for Living*. Glendale, California: G/L Publications, 1976.

Douglass, Merrill E. and Donna N. Douglass. *Manage Your Time Your Work Yourself: The Updated Edition*. New York: AMACOM, 1993.

Ellwood, Mark. *Cut the Glut of E-Mail*. Toronto: Pace Productivity, 2002.

Flynn, Nancy and Randolph Kahn. *E-Mail Rules: A Business Guide to Managing Policies, Security, and Legal Issues, for E-Mail and Digital Communications*. New York: AMACOM, 2003.

Gleeson, Kerry. *The Personal Efficiency Program: How to Get Organized to Do More Work in Less Time*. New York: John Wiley & Sons, 2000.

Hutchings, Patricia J. *Managing Workplace Chaos: Solutions for Handling Information, Paper, Time, and Stress*. New York: AMACOM, 2002.

Izzo, John B. and Pam Withers. *Values Shift: The New Work Ethic and What It Means for Business*. Toronto: Prentice Hall Canada.

Jensen, Bill. *Simplicity: The New Competitive Advantage in a World of More, Better, Faster*. Cambridge, Massachusetts: Perseus Publishing, 2000.

Kieffer, George David. *The Strategy of Meetings*. New York: Simon & Schuster, 1988.

Lewis, David. *10-Minute Time and Stress Management: How to Gain an 'Extra' 10 Hours a Week!* London: Judy Piatkus, 1995.

Macdonald, Gordon. *Restoring Your Spiritual Passion*. Nashville: Thomas Nelson, 1986.

Morgenstern, Julie. *Time Management from the Inside Out: the Foolproof System for Taking Control of Your Schedule – and Your Life*. New York: Henry Holt and Company, 2000.

Moxham, Richard. *Taming Time: a Practical Guide to Time Management*. London: Spiro Press, 2001.

Pollar, Odette. *Organizing Your Workspace: a Guide to Personal Productivity*. Revised ed. Los Altos, California: Crisp Publications, 1999.

Roberts-Phelps, Graham. *Telephone Tactics*. London: Hawksmere, 1999.

Shenk, David. Data Smog: *Surviving the Information Glut*. New York: HarperCollins, 1997.

Silver, Susan. *Organized to Be Your Best! Simplify and Improve How You Work*. [Los Angeles]: Adams-Hall Publishing, 2000.

St. James, Elaine. *Simplify Your Work Life: Ways to Change the Way You Work So You Have More Time to Live*. New York: Hyperion, 2001.

Stack, Laura. *Leave the Office Earlier: The Productivity Pro Shows You How to Do More in Less Time...and Feel Great About It*. New York: Broadway Books, 2004.

Streibel, Barbara J. *The Manager's Guide to Effective Meetings*. New York: McGraw Hill, 2003.

Swenson, Richard A. *Margin: How to Create the Emotional, Physical, Financial, and Time Reserves You Need*. Colorado Springs, Colorado: Navpress, 1992.

Swenson, Richard A. *The Overload Syndrome: Learning to Live within Your Limits*. Colorado Springs, Colorado: Navpress, 1998.

Trout, Jack and Steve Rivkin. *The Power of Simplicity: A Management Guide to Cutting through the Nonsense and Doing Things Right*. New York: McGraw-Hill, 1999.

Winston, Stephanie. *Getting Out from Under: Redefining Your Priorities in an Overwhelming World: A Powerful Program for Personal Change*. Reading, Massachusetts: Perseus Books, 1999.

Winston, Stephanie. *The Organized Executive: The Classic Program for Productivity: New Ways to Manage Time, Paper, People, and the Digital Office*. New York: Warner Books, 2001.

Ziglar, Zig. *See You at the Top*. Gretna, Louisiana: Pelican Publishing Company, 2000.

PERIODICALS

Bolan, Sandra. "Stress-Free IT Professionals But, End-Users Are Buckling Under the Pressure of Technology Overload." *Computing Canada* (16 November 2001): 26.

Brooks, David. "Time to Do Everything except Think." *Newsweek* (30 April 2001): 71

Brokaw, Leslie. "The Model Meeting Agenda." *Inc.* (July 1994): 77.

Bruce, Dennis. "Information. Had Enough Lately?" *Marketing* (8 October 2001): 26.

Conrath, Chris. "Welcome to the Overload: Today's Workers Are Being Swamped by an Information Deluge, But Are Slowly Learning to Cope." *Computerworld Canada* (3 November 2000): 42.

Kaye, Steve. "How to Handle Interruptions That Steal Your Time." *Canadian Manager* (Summer 1999): 25.

Kaye, Steve. "Managing Monsters in Meetings: How to Stop Unproductive Behavior." *Canadian Manager* (Fall 1998): 14.

Kiechel, Walter. "Overscheduled, and Not Loving It." *Fortune* (8 April 1991): 105.

McGinn, Daniel. "Mired in Meetings." *Newsweek* (16 October 2000): 52.

McKenna, Patrick J. and David H. Maister. "Energize Your Meetings." *Canadian Manager* (Winter 2003): 23.

Sibley, Kathleen. "Communications Overload Is Hindering Work: Study." *Computing Canada* (26 May 1997): 6.

Taylor, Harold. "Don't Let E-Mail Ruin Communications." *Mississauga Business Times* July 2001: 34.

Taylor, Harold. "Managing Your Paperwork. (Taming the Paper Tiger Software)." *Canadian Manager* (Fall 1998): 20.

NEWSPAPERS

Boyd, Robert S. "Information Overload Is Swamping the Planet." *The Gazette Montreal* (22 February 2004): D6.

Cordon, Sandra. "Coping with Rising Employee Stress: More Companies Provide Help to Keep Overwhelmed Workers Productive." *The Gazette Montreal* (13 September 1999): F2.

Faulkner, Rob. "What Would Hamlet Think? Pop Index; We're Creating More Information Than We Can Handle." *The Spectator Hamilton* (8 November 2003): G26.

Kirklighter, Kirk. "I Think, Therefore I Am…Inundated; Along with Benefits, Information Explosion Brings More Stress into Our Lives." *Toronto Star* (27 July 2001): D4.

Lightman, Alan. "Prisoners of the Wired World: Technology Was Supposed to Make Us Free: Instead, It Has Enslaved Us." *Globe & Mail* (16 March 2002): NA.

Rice-Oxley, Mark. "Weary of the Rat Race, Time to 'Downshift', Mate! Britons -- the Workaholics of Europe – Take Lower-Paying Jobs in Their Quest for Simpler, More Fulfilling Lives." *The Spectator Hamilton* (24 January 2004): F12.

Rifkin, Jeremy. "The Perils of 24/7: Is Our Nanosecond Culture Enslaving Us Rather Than Making Life Easier?" *The Gazette Montreal* (4 June 2001): B3.

Sankey, Derek. "Information Overload: Overcoming Productivity Hurdles in the Face of Expanding Technology." *Calgary Herald* (2 September 2000): W1.

"Technology Taking Our Free Time Away." *Daily News Halifax, N.S.* (20 December 1999): 19.

Whittaker, Stephanie. "Employee E-mail Overload: Communications Tool a Boon for Businesses But a Burden for Workers." *The Gazette Montreal* (5 August 2000): 11.

INDEX

R

S

T